S0-AGW-276

About the One Earth Books

During its nearly one hundred years of educating the public about environmental issues, the National Audubon Society has rarely achieved anything as important as reaching out to the world's young people, the voices of tomorrow. For Audubon and its 600,000 members, nothing is so crucial as ensuring that those voices speak in the future on behalf of wildlife.

Audubon reaches out to people in many ways—through its nationwide system of wildlife sanctuaries, through research vital to helping set the nation's environmental policy, through lobbying for sound conservation laws, through television documentaries and fact-based dramatic films, through *Audubon* magazine and computer software, and through ecology workshops for adults and Audubon Adventures clubs in school classrooms. Each of these is critical to reaching a large audience. And now, with the Audubon One Earth books, the environmental community can speak to the young minds in our citizenry.

Audubon is proud to publish One Earth in cooperation with Delacorte Press. In addition to bringing new information and experiences to young readers, these books will instill in them a fundamental concern for the environment and its decline at the hands of humanity. They will also, it is hoped, stimulate an undying interest in the natural world that will empower young people, as they mature, to protect the world's natural wonders for themselves and for future generations.

We at Audubon hope you will enjoy the One Earth books and that you will find in them an inspiration for joining our earth-saving mission. Young people are the hope for our future.

Christopher N. Palmer
Executive Editor
President, National Audubon
Society Productions

ONE EARTH

SAVE OUR OCEANS AND COASTS

RON HIRSCHI

Photographs by Erwin and Peggy Bauer and others

National
Audubon
Society

DELACORTE PRESS/NEW YORK

For my cousin Tom,
who taught me more than anyone
about life in the sea.

If you would like to receive more information about the
National Audubon Society write to:

National Audubon Society, Membership Department
700 Broadway, New York, New York 10003

Executive Editor: Christopher N. Palmer
Special thanks to Roger DiSilvestro.

Published by
Delacorte Press
Bantam Doubleday Dell Publishing Group, Inc.
1540 Broadway
New York, New York 10036

Library of Congress Cataloging in Publication Data
Hirschi, Ron.
Save our oceans and coasts / Ron Hirschi ; photographs by
Erwin and Peggy Bauer and others.
p.   cm.—(One earth)
"National Audubon Society."
Summary: Discusses the characteristics, animal life, and
importance of oceans and coastal areas and ways to protect these
habitats.
ISBN 0-385-31077-3
0-385-31126-5 (pbk)
1. Ocean—Juvenile literature.   2. Coast changes—Juvenile
literature. 3. Marine ecology—Juvenile literature.   [1. Ocean.
2. Coast changes. 3. Marine ecology. 4. Ecology. 5. Environmental
protection.] I. Bauer, Erwin A., ill. II. Bauer, Peggy, ill.
III. Title. IV. Series: Hirschi, Ron. One earth.
GC21.5.H57   1993
574.5'2636—dc20   92-37384
CIP
AC
This edition is published simultaneously in Delacorte Press hardcover and
paperback editions.

Manufactured in the United States of America

December 1993

10 9 8 7 6 5 4 3 2 1

MVA

Contents

Introduction vi
Forested Shorelines 1
Rocky Coasts 16
Islands and Nesting Beaches 28
Open Sea 36
Coral Reefs 49
Coastal Wetlands and Soft Sandy Shores 55
Afterword 68
Index 70

ONE EARTH

Introduction

Just as the sea turtle is tied to the land, your life is connected to the sea—no matter where you live. Even if you have never smelled fresh sea air, watched a puffin feed its young, or listened to the humpback whale's beautiful song, there is a lot the ocean offers you. And there is a lot you can do in return to save our oceans.

Most ocean dwellers are connected to many habitats and need lots of different areas to survive. Seabirds, for instance, find food out on the open sea, but they must also have islands for nesting places. Schools of fish hatch and grow in shallow coastal bays, often right at the very edge of the beach. Others begin life in tiny mountain streams, then spend their adult life hundreds of miles offshore, where whales also swim the open sea. Even some whales live near the shore. Gray whales spend most of their lives in shallow coastal waters and even swim into rivers and small, calm inlets.

Oceans are vital to all life, and so, too, are their coasts. Therefore, much of this book focuses on the coastal zone—the broad area that includes both land and sea. You will read about animals living along ocean shores that stretch thousands of miles from Maine to Texas, from Alaska to California and beyond, and along the shores of the several thousand islands that dot the sea. You will also explore the rich forests of kelp, lush seagrass communities, and highly productive coastal marshes, since each of these habitats helps support fish, birds, marine mammals, and other ocean life.

We hope that much of what you learn will inspire you to

help the fragile and valuable coastal areas, and to do all that you can to help stop the threats the deeper sea faces, too. These threats include spilled oil, discarded plastic, the disposal of sewage and toxic wastes, and the harvesting of far too many fish to sustain our greed. Even if you live in the middle of the United States, rivers and streams near your home connect you to the ocean. You can make sure those rivers and streams carry only clean water to the sea.

While no one can expect you to save the oceans single-handedly, maybe you can help by embracing the needs of gentle whales and sea turtles, cleaning up a riverbank or beach, and recycling or refusing to use plastics that may become ocean pollutants. One continuous and ever-connected ocean ecosystem is all we have. Its wondrous waters are yours to save.

Forested Shorelines

Since so many people live along our coasts, it is not surprising that the species dependent on coastal zone habitats are the most endangered faces of the sea. Island, wetland, and reef life are severely affected by human activity. So, too, is the narrow strip of firm ground that rims the ocean shore. Once much of this shore was an undisturbed coastal forest. Now coastal forests have nearly vanished. What was once a nesting place for bald eagles, herons, and osprey is currently home to an increasing number of people. If we are to become a more active part of the coastal community, we must gain a better understanding of this world and the lives of the animal and plant species that were here before us.

When nonnative people, for instance, first arrived on the shores of North America, they were met with a wall of trees that must have appeared to be marching into the sea. The land was covered with towering forests that have been almost completely removed and replaced by human structures. Today very few natural forested shores remain, but where they do, as along the Pacific Northwest coast, these areas provide us with some of the most spectacular of all habitats.

Occasionally, trees in the coastal zone still fall into the sea, actually becoming an important part of the coastal ecology. Baby salmon and other fish hide beneath these trees. Herons rest on the trunks, barnacles attach to the fallen branches, and otters make their dens at the base of the trees, just as they do along the banks of a stream.

Drifting along shorelines, big trunks and root wads from

1

fallen trees stack up to form a line of defense against crashing waves. The roots of shoreline trees that still stand, like the roots of trees along a riverbank, help keep soil from washing swiftly into tidal waters. Sadly, we have replaced much of our shoreline trees with concrete bulkheads, docks, piers, and other walls of rock and cut timbers.

THE COASTAL ZONE

The coastal zone is not simply the edge of the sea where waves wash the shore. It includes other broad regions where both land and water habitats affect one another in many ways. One of the clearest examples of the complex beauty of this critical zone is an *estuary.*

Estuaries are places where rivers meet the sea. Chesapeake Bay, Puget Sound, and San Francisco Bay are large estuaries and extremely rich bodies of water that have supported human communities for several thousand years. People harvest the riches of these and other estuaries, often depleting their populations of birds, mammals, and fish. At the same time, people have destroyed the fragile edges of the estuary — the wetlands that are the food base for virtually all the organisms living there.

Estuary wetlands include salt marsh, seagrass, and algae. These and other plants growing in the wetlands become food in many ways, for many mouths. Marine animals eat the plants directly.

But they also consume the marsh grasses, seagrasses, and algae indirectly as they break into small pieces and begin to decay. This broken-down plant matter, known as *detritus,* is quickly covered with bacteria. Like peanut butter spread on bread, detritus is a nutritious seafood sandwich. It might not sound too appetizing to us, but the detritivores (animals that eat the stuff) love it. Detritivores include mussels, clams, oysters, marine worms, and marine amphipods. Amphipods are little, shrimplike animals that are food for fish, birds, and other marine life-forms. But they are also the favorite food of small fish known as sculpins. There are many kinds of marine sculpins, including the staghorn, named for the little antlerlike bones that stick out along its head.

Staghorn sculpins swim a little way up rivers and streams, and not very far out to sea. They and other small sculpin relatives are eaten by otters, loons, goldeneye ducks, sea anemones, herring, great blue herons, bald eagles,

osprey, pigeon guillemots, harlequin ducks, Bonaparte's gulls, glaucous-winged gulls, lingcod, coho salmon, cutthroat trout, starfish, crabs, other sculpins, red-necked grebes, and raccoons. Like large insects, seeds, and berries in a forest community, the sculpin and other small fish are at the heart of important food webs that sustain lots of animals. We may not see the sculpins often, but we do see the ocean dwellers that need them for breakfast, lunch, or dinner. They are all tied together in the economy of the shore. Sculpins are an excellent example of the importance of the detritus food pathways originating in our estuaries. They eat the marine amphipods that eat the detritus that grew in the marsh that lives in the coastal wetlands that rim the shore of the estuary.

To understand the full value of the coastal wetlands within estuaries and other shallow coastal zone habitats, think of them as cafes and restaurants for all of the eagles, fish, and whales along the shore.

Deforested shorelines or those with smaller trees are now more common than those with standing ancient forest. We have learned about the importance of these trees at great expense as we have watched our homes, roadways, bridges, and other structures topple into the sea, just as trees did before them. Shorelines are dynamic. They change constantly, like the path of a river, like the sand on a beach. Sometimes change happens overnight when hurricanes or tidal waves sweep our buildings away. But shoreline change is usually more gradual.

Like all natural systems, the forested shoreline exchanges pieces of itself with other places. It's almost as if the edge of the sea were an enormous sand castle lined with trees to keep the entire structure from disappearing. But like any sand castle, the edges crumble eventually. And the pieces of the shore, including the trees, are swept away to become part of the sea. Somewhere on the ocean floor a crab is hiding beneath a piece of a giant fir tree that toppled last winter.

Forests at the edge of the sea in many southeastern areas offer us similar examples of how closely linked the sea and trees can become. Perhaps you have read about their mangrove forests—coastal woodlands that seem to walk out into the ocean on leglike trunks. The extensive root system of the mangrove props the tree up, allowing seawater to flow around the trunk. These roots trap leaves, seaweed, and other food sources, creating a rich coastal soup. This feeding place is one of the many important feeding areas within our coastal zone. Sea trout, shrimp, spiny lobsters, and many other sea creatures depend on the mangrove for their food supply and for far more.

Where mangrove forests are protected, the trees form a close relationship with the seagrass beds and coral reefs that lie offshore. Trees act as natural buffers against the sea's erosive forces. They also shelter small fish beneath their twisting trunks and roots as if they were grandparents hugging little grandkids.

Sadly, mangrove forests have been cleared during road construction, shoreline house building, and dock or seawall installation all along the Florida coast. Now silt once trapped by their roots washes over and smothers the rich seagrass beds and coral reefs lying offshore. The harmony between land and sea is upset, destroying rich feeding grounds and nursery areas for baby fish and other wildlife.

Even in those places where trees do not actually wet their toes in ocean sand, such as along most of our northern

COASTAL ZONE CHANGES

Changes to the shoreline occur when wind and water erode and transport pieces of the land, beach, and seafloor. They occur when steep, sandy bluffs crumble, when tides and wind-driven water stir up beach sand and carry it to new locations, or when new sand, silt, and stone wash into the sea from rivers. The coast advances in some places, retreats in others. A quick trip around the lower 48 states provides clues to both natural change and change brought on by human interference with our shores and rivers.

SOME HISTORIC CHANGES
INCLUDE:
• Cliffs at Shannon Point in western Washington retreated more than 15 feet between 1893 and 1969, primarily because of natural erosion.
• The Nooksack River delta advanced almost a kilometer into the Strait of Georgia near Bel-

lingham, Washington, between 1906 and 1961.
• Broad, sandy beaches north of the mouth of the Columbia River are advancing as stream-borne sediment flows into the Pacific Ocean and is swept alongshore for more than 25 miles as it builds the Long Beach Peninsula.
• Columbia River sediments also built beaches to the south, along the coast of Oregon, but changes have occurred following jetty and dam construction on the river. Sediment trapped behind the many dams on the Columbia is thought to be responsible for erosion at Clatsop Spit, an area that was advancing into the sea before the dams.
• About two thirds of the California coast is steep cliff or rocky shore, and about 85 percent of the shore actively erodes, but very slowly.

• San Francisco Bay has changed because of natural sediments' washing into it from the Sacramento and San Joaquin rivers. But dramatic change has been due to human influences. The bay has shrunk over the past 200 years, being reduced from 1,800 to 1,100 square kilometers. Tons of sediment flowed into San Francisco Bay when miners washed away hillsides in the Sierra Nevada Mountains as they searched for gold. And most of the bay's wetlands have been filled or otherwise cut off from the sea in recent years.
• Near Los Angeles, construction of breakwaters and piers causes beaches to advance on one side of the structures and to erode on the other.
• Erosion at Newport Beach, California, has occurred in recent years as the result of dam construction on the Santa Ana River.

shores, the balance between forest and ocean is delicate. There the balance may not be as visible or well understood, perhaps because the roots of northern trees grow in slightly firmer ground than the mangroves. Perhaps we have also lost our memory of how vital the connections were between forested shorelines and the sea in the not too distant past—when coastal trees towered high and were far more extensive than they are today.

Bald eagles, great blue herons, marbled murrelets, and

- Near San Diego, jetty construction has modified the shoreline, but new sand is moved to the shore by people as deeper parts of the seafloor are dredged.
- The Texas shoreline has changed because of human interference, as seen most dramatically at the mouth of the Rio Brazos. Until about 1938 the natural delta at the river mouth moved out into the Gulf of Mexico. An artificial channel was cut, moving the river mouth, and a new delta grew into the sea more than a mile in 20 years. The old delta has been cut into smaller pieces by wave action.
- The immense and complex Mississippi delta has been severely affected by flood control structures along the river that trap sediment that once entered the Gulf of Mexico. Some local areas still advance, but many, such as the shores of Grand Isle, erode. Recent estimates are that the delta loses one meter per hundred years.

- Pensacola Beach, Florida, loses about one meter each year, and several other Florida shores are also moving landward. These include St. Vincent Island and the western shore of St. Joseph Point.
- Along mangrove shores of Florida's southwestern coast, the beach advances at times, then is altered by hurricane forces.
- Atlantic shores of Florida change during hurricanes. They are also affected by jetty construction, as seen near Miami, where beach sands can build up on the northern side of artificial structures and erode to the south.
- Cape Canaveral has eroded on its northeastern side and advanced along the southern shore.
- Within Chesapeake Bay, marshlands have been advancing, especially at river mouths, where marsh plants trap sediment and where new wetland plants take root, grow, and move the land seaward.

- Pieces of the New Jersey shore have eroded, others have advanced, but the pattern of change has been extensively modified by people. For example, sections of Sandy Hook erode as new sediment is added artificially. And other sections of the shoreline are modified with rock and concrete walls.
- A historical study of Martha's Vineyard traced change from 1776 to 1969 and reported a continuing process of erosion such as on the barrier at Katama Bay, where the shoreline was cut back about 3,000 feet since our country was born. Near Martha's Vineyard, other areas, such as Monomoy Island, advanced.
- One of the least-changed shorelines along the entire coast of the United States meets the Atlantic in Maine. The rocky shores of our northeasternmost state have remained almost unchanged in the past hundred years.

many of the forest trees themselves, such as Sitka spruce, are just a few of the threatened faces in today's forested shorelines. Let's look closer at their lives. Perhaps then we can find ways to help save them.

Bald Eagles

There are many types of eagles living along the world's coasts, including African fishing eagles; white-tailed sea eagles, which barely survive in western Europe; Steller's sea eagles, which hunt along the coast of Korea and Siberia; and white-bellied sea eagles, which fly along the shores of Australia and India. Then, of course, there is the bald eagle, which is the very symbol of our nation.

Although threatened, especially along the eastern forested shorelines, bald eagles can still be seen making dramatic dives from the sky. They prey on sea gulls once in a while and often eat the eggs of these abundant coastal birds. They also dine on ducks, rockfish, salmon, flounders, and puffins, as well as other seabirds of the open ocean. Eagles often scavenge food such as dead fish or the bodies of marine mammals washed in with the tide. For many centuries the eagle's habit of eating dead animals along the beach was safe.

But oil spills have since turned eagle food habits into a deadly game.

When oil spills into the ocean, seabirds, sea otters, and other marine animals die. Their oil-caked bodies wash ashore. Unfortunately, hungry eagles are unaware of the threat these oil-soaked animals pose. They see these bodies merely as easy meals. Even if an eagle were to pull off the feathers of an oil-soaked bird before eating it, chances are good that some oil would stick to the eagle's own feathers in the process.

Once on the eagle's feathers, oil prevents them from acting as insulation from rain and cold. Without such insulation it isn't long before the eagle dies of exposure—if it hasn't

When we *endanger places* such as the shoreline forest, we *endanger faces* such as the condor, osprey, eagle, and marbled murrelet. And these faces are connected to many other *places* — such as rivers, mountains, the open sea, rocky shores, and coastal wetlands — and to many other *faces* — such as whales, seals, salmon, shorebirds, trees, and kelp.

Think of the connections between places and faces as a puzzle. Habitats, such as the coastal zone or the open sea, are the puzzle board, the plants and animals that live there are the pieces. Now imagine placing these pieces on a board that is ever shifting because of our actions.

Understanding how to keep all the pieces in place requires an understanding of connections. To make sure all the pieces remain in place, we must keep the board intact — we must take care of our seas. We can begin by protecting habitats on land — in our own backyards.

already died from oil it has eaten accidentally. Death rates are highest when eagles swallow the oil. And when they carry oil-soaked prey back to their nests, their young make some of the same fatal mistakes.

Pollutants other than oil also affect eagles and other coastal fish eaters, such as osprey. Pesticides concentrated in marine food webs build up as little fish are eaten by big fish. When an eagle eats a fish with high levels of certain chemicals in its body, the eagle can no longer reproduce. One of the clearest examples of this was the use of the pesticide DDT by many farmers.

After DDT was sprayed on crops, it washed into streams, lakes, and coastal waters. It worked its way into the bodies of fish through food webs, where the chemical broke down, but only slowly. Eagles that ate contaminated fish laid eggs whose shells were too thin to hatch successfully.

Fortunately, DDT was banned in the United States in 1972, thanks to the public opposition that mounted after Rachel Carson wrote a book on the subject called SILENT SPRING. Since DDT's banning, the number of eagles in the United States has increased. Today the largest nesting concentrations of eagles can be found along the forested shorelines of the Pacific Northwest. Here they may be safe from DDT, but new threats have already begun to affect these magnificent birds.

Bald eagles are not small birds. Their body is about the size of a kindergartener. Their wingspan can stretch to nearly eight feet. No surprise, then, that eagles need incredibly big trees to support their nest and their family members. An eagle nest is made of sticks gathered by both parents. This huge mass of limbs and branches is added to each year and can weigh more than a ton. Some have been measured as wide as 12 feet and as deep as eight feet.

Aside from big trees to hold their enormous nests, eagles need relatively quiet places free from human disturbance. Too much noise, boat traffic, or other activities interrupt an eagle's ability to feed its young. As a result, many baby eagles do not grow big enough to fly safely from their shoreline nests.

Good news and bad news for eagles can be seen in historical trends. In 1974 there were fewer than 800 known nesting pairs in the United States south of Alaska. By 1990 efforts to restore their numbers helped them to increase (largely because of the banning of DDT) to more than 2,600 pairs. In addition to DDT elimination in the United States, eagle recovery has been helped by education, research, and relocation of eagle nestlings and eagle eggs to new nesting areas. But eagles are not doing well in all corners of our country.

A look at the past helps show us how changes in the forested shoreline affected eagle populations. The majority of nesting eagles in the United States today live on the west coast, but in 1903 Frank Chapman, a man who spent a lot of time studying birds, wrote that eagles were more common near the Atlantic coast. This was true largely because they didn't have much of a home out west as shoreline forests toppled during the days when the West was being settled.

At the same time that many of the forests along the Pacific coast were being cleared, trees that had been cut on the east coast during the earliest days of American colonization were growing back. As a result, eagles and other birds were able to find more homes in Atlantic woodlands.

Today, as more and more people move to the wooded corners of Maine and other forested Atlantic shorelines, history begins to repeat itself, displacing eagles and other wildlife from shoreline forests. The sad truth is that, even though eagle numbers in general are increasing nationwide, the birds are in trouble on both coasts of the United States. This is especially true in the rapidly changing coastal areas of the state of Washington, where shoreline trees are cut and waterfront cleared in eagle nesting areas. Shoreline trees are sometimes replaced, but new trees are cut almost as quickly as they grow without enough time for eagles to claim them for nests. Since people move into newly cleared areas to live, the eagles get few chances to put a bid in for their own waterfront home.

If you would like to help eagles, there are lots of things you can do. The U.S. Fish and Wildlife Service hopes to reach a goal of 2,700 nesting pairs of bald eagles by the year 2000. This is a rather low number, considering the historic populations of our national bird. Maybe if you create projects or work with other eagle-saving organizations, you could urge the FWS to set its sights higher, and perhaps more eagles will survive.

Eagle populations like those in coastal Washington (SEE PAGE 10) allow a maximum of one nesting pair per mile of forested shoreline. Eagles don't really like other birds' hunting in their nesting area in the summertime. It interferes with their own ability to catch enough fish and other food to feed their young. To protect the eagles successfully, we will need to make sure these shoreline nesting territories are defended against human encroachment. Some activities are tolerated within the one-mile area, but if you have the chance to watch nesting eagles, keep track of new clearing or other disturbances and report them to your state wildlife agency.

The immediate nesting area and eagle nest trees need

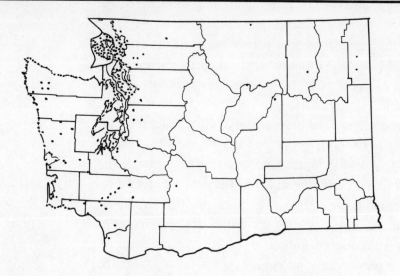

DID YOU KNOW?

The highest concentrations of nesting bald eagles south of Alaska are in Florida, Wisconsin, Minnesota, and Washington. The importance of shoreline forests is clear from this map, in which every black dot along the Pacific coast and the shores of inland marine waters of Washington represents an eagle nest in a large tree within a forested segment of the shore. The majority of other nesting sites are along rivers.

Eagle biologists estimate that the number of bald eagles nationwide once reached at least 100,000 and probably more. Today there are only about 5,000 nesting in the entire lower 48 states.

Bald eagle food habits connect them to many ocean habitats, including the open sea. The remains of as many as 30 sea gulls have been found in a single eagle nest. Bald eagles also feed on marine fish, including herring, salmon, rockfish, flounders, and sculpins. And they consume seabirds and seabird eggs, as well as the beached remains of marine mammals.

The most serious threat to nesting bald eagles is the destruction of shoreline forests.

Bald eagle populations in Florida have grown at about 10 percent each year. But Florida's human population grows at a much faster pace. Incredibly, 1,000 people a day are added to the already overpopulated state. More people mean more habitat losses for ea-gles, especially along the coast and along busy highways. In fact, many eagles are killed each year on Florida highways as they fly down to feed on roadkills.

In the Chesapeake Bay, eagle nesting success (the number of baby eagles that leave the nest healthy, compared with the number of eggs laid) has fallen significantly in recent years. Scientists blame habitat loss along the shores of the bay and increased human activity near nests.

Increased boat traffic, for instance, threatens eagles and other species. Eagles are especially affected by boating activity during the nesting season, when adults are frightened from feeding areas as they try to catch food for their young.

Source: Washington Department of Wildlife.

formal protection, protection you might be surprised to learn they lack under existing laws. It is actually legal to destroy eagle nesting habitat, and virtually no protection is given to eagles' food supply or their feeding areas in the sea. It is also legal to destroy valuable eagle wintering sites. They will lose these valuable wintering places, which are often single, scattered large trees along the coast, unless we begin to put eagle winter sites on maps. You can help with this effort, educating others about the importance of these places. You can also help encourage legislation to protect eagle nests, eagle feeding habitat, and eagle wintering sites.

Write your representatives in Congress and the state legislature, urging them to protect the habitat eagles need to survive. If we can't save the home of our nation's symbol, will we be able to save any land for the many other plants and animals that need our help? If we can't save the shoreline forests nearest our homes, can we save any piece of the sea?

Participate in eagle censuses during nesting time and during the winter, even if you live far from the coast. Eagles that nest next to the sea will move inland, bringing a part of the ocean world near your home. And if no census exists in your area, begin one, as students have done in Heath, Ohio. Fifth-grade students in Heath started what may be the first eagle-saving organization begun by young people. Known as Eagle Geographics, this group is urging that all reports of wintering eagles in their state be mailed to them in care of IN OUR HANDS, Wickliffe School, 2405 Wickliffe Road, Columbus, Ohio 43221.

If you locate an eagle nest, contact your state wildlife agency or local Audubon Society. If you want to become involved in national winter bald eagle counts, contact the research division or nongame biologist in your state's wildlife agency. Since 1979 many states have participated in a winter bald eagle census, a count that has greatly helped us to understand where eagles spend their time after the nesting

The 1980 U.S. census reported that 52 percent of all people in our country lived within coastal areas. By the year 2000, that figure is expected to reach 80 percent if current trends continue. This increase poses a serious threat to bald eagles, herons, osprey, spoonbills, marbled murrelets, and other coastal wildlife.

Buffer zones are critical for nesting wildlife and for the resting, breeding, and feeding areas of coastal birds and mammals. Consider the buffer or comfort zone of these animals as you approach them by boat or as you walk along the shoreline.

Keep in mind that even if you live far from the sea, many of your day-to-day activities affect the quality of ocean water. If you live near a river, pollutants that wash off the roads, lawns, and parking lots of your town eventually wash into the sea. Sewage dumped into the sea and other wastes often wash up onto beaches, too. Much of that waste is needlessly produced and thoughtlessly disposed of rather than reused, recycled, or refused in the first place.

In an attempt to control trash dumping at sea, a 1988 worldwide ban prohibits disposal of plastic debris from ships. Wouldn't it be great to prohibit the disposal of plastic from land, as well?

The hope in banning plastic disposal from ships is to eliminate the 14 billion pounds of plastic and other waste lost or discarded every year from pleasure and commercial boats, ships, and barges. If you see any waste being thrown overboard or dumped into the ocean, call the U.S. Coast Guard and report the violators. If you see waste being thrown into the rivers or lakes near your home, contact your state or local environmental protection agency. If no law protects your local waters, join with local environmental groups to discover new ways to protect your water's quality.

In 1989, 65,000 people walked the nation's beaches in an attempt to pick up the trash along about 3,000 miles of shoreline. They were able to collect about a million pieces of plastic and foam trash. Much of this plastic did not litter the shores during your parents' childhood days; disposable lighters, plastic forks, plastic bags, plastic milk bottles, plastic pop containers, and plastic trash bags are recent inventions. Do we need them at all?

season. Maybe you will help locate a winter roosting forest near your home, out along the forested ocean shore.

Great Blue Herons

"When we try to pick out anything by itself, we find it hitched to everything else in the universe."—John Muir

This seems especially true of great blue herons, which are hitched to almost every coast in North America. As a matter of fact, they are about as connected to all of us and the sea as any other bird or mammal. While great blue herons live near the ocean, they also live in the middle of the country.

To help with future beach cleanups, some plastic-recycling companies have made efforts to join hands with volunteers involved in trash collection. A New York company has made plastic lumber from trash collected in 1990 on the Chesapeake Bay. Park benches made from the plastic will be donated by the company and installed at cleanup locations along the shores of the bay.

If you want to volunteer for annual beach cleanups in your state, contact the CENTER FOR MARINE CONSERVATION, 1725 Desales Street NW, Suite 500, Washington, DC 20036. Phone: 202-429-5609. If you do not live along the coast, organize a river or stream cleanup.

In September 1988 a federal law was passed to require the use of degradable beverage containers nationwide. The law directed the U.S. Environmental Protection Agency to develop regulations to implement the law within two years. To date, the EPA has not acted. But even if the degradable containers were available, much of the plastic in them would not really disappear, since "degradable" plastic lasts for many, many years, if not centuries.

Monofilament fishing line is often thrown away and adds to the deadly list of plastic debris that kills marine wildlife. Berkley, a fishing tackle manufacturer, is working to decrease the problems associated with its fishing-line products and those of other manufacturers. Berkley provides free bins to stores and will pay to transport fishing line to recycling centers. Line is then recycled into stove knobs, boat propellers, and backpack fasteners. For more information, contact Jan Bowles at BERKLEY, 1 Berkley Drive, Spirit Lake, Iowa 52360. Phone: 712-336-1520.

The most abundant items reported during the 1989 national beach cleanup were cigarette filters, foam plastic (Styrofoam), paper, glass, plastic food bags, wrappers, metal beverage containers, plastic caps and lids, plastic straws, plastic eating utensils, and glass bottles (states with bottle bills, requiring deposits, were not listed among those with the highest number of bottles present). A total of 2,502,230 items were picked up in the above categories.

They like to hang out by rivers, along little streams, and in ponds, as well as down by the sea. Like eagles, they prefer to nest in trees. Unlike eagles, they like to nest in the company of lots of friends and relatives. A big heron nesting place, or *rookery*, might house more than a hundred nesting pairs of these elegant birds.

Tall and lanky, the great blue heron would be a center for the Los Angeles Lakers or the Chicago Bulls if human. These birds are graceful in flight, efficient as fisherbirds, and a welcome sight for people living along the coast. Bluish gray, these four-foot-high wading birds wear black-and-white crested crowns of feathers on their slender heads.

Great blue herons almost always appear to be hunched over, silently stalking their prey. Standing knee-deep in water, they wait for fish to come near. With a quick and skillful motion, they snatch pipefish, flounders, sculpins, and an occasional crab from shallow water, from a floating platform of kelp, or from tree trunks that allow them to fish in deeper water.

LARGE WADING BIRDS

Great blue herons are one of many large wading birds living along the coast. Several others are not so common. They include the following:

	HABITAT	FOOD CONNECTIONS	THREATS
Roseate spoonbill	Nests in mangroves and other coastal trees and shrubs Feeds in shallow coastal wetlands	Shrimp and small fish	Destruction of nesting habitat; filling, dredging, and other loss of coastal wetlands
Glossy ibis	Nests in low trees or shrubs growing in water Feeds in marshy shallows, salt marsh, and tidal channels	Fiddler crabs, insects, and snakes	Destruction of nesting habitat
Louisiana heron	Nests, sometimes in colonies of as many as 1,000, in mangroves, buttonwood, or low shrubs and marsh grass Wades in shallows	Small fish and marine invertebrates	Wetland destruction and loss of nesting habitat
Whooping crane	Nests in Canadian interior Feeds during winter in salt marshes of coastal Texas	Small fish and marine invertebrates that, in turn, feed on marsh plants, directly or indirectly (but also eats wetland plants)	Loss of wetlands from Canada to Texas, both along the ocean shore and along its migratory route in the middle of America
Snowy egret	Nests in trees or shrubs near fresh as well as salt water. Feeds in freshwater marsh and salt marsh	Small fish and marine invertebrates, including shrimp	One of the many birds saved from extinction when a ban was placed on killing it for its beautiful feathers; now can be as abundant as in former times only with protection of wetlands
Reddish egret	Nests in mangroves or other trees near salt water Feeds in shallow bays and in other coastal marine waters, but is not common, occurring in Florida and Texas along the Gulf Coast	Fish, crabs, and other animals dependent on mangrove and marsh food base	Destruction of wetlands and nesting habitat

Because they are widely distributed, from Alaska to South America, great blue herons are strong indicators of the health of our coastal ecosystems. But the fact that they are so spread out can be quite deceptive. Because there are frequent sightings of these birds we tend not to notice that their overall population is thinning. As ornithologist Ralph Palmer says, "The great blue heron is holding its own. Except locally." In other words, the great blue heron may not be in danger of becoming extinct, but it is in danger, especially in many coastal locations where forested shorelines are disappearing. Sadly, not many people are paying attention to this loss.

Few organizations, if any, have ever been created with the single purpose of saving the great blue heron. Maybe you could be among the first to start a heron-saving organization.

Observations made in the Puget Sound region of Washington State may offer some explanations as to why great blue herons are disappearing from the coastline. Puget Sound is an inland sea fed by lots of rivers and streams. Estuarine feeding areas are great fishing spots for herons, and the birds usually have no trouble finding enough to eat. They do have a hard time, though, finding a place to raise their kids.

Great blue heron nesting grounds are in trouble. Herons are rather shy birds around their nests. Like bald eagles, they require a buffer zone of undisturbed land between them and most forms of human activity. For the same reasons that we put fences around our yards or put up that invisible wall between ourselves and people we don't want near us, great blue herons need these buffer zones. But the sad truth is that their buffer zones aren't respected by many people. Sadder still is that in most states there is little or no legal protection to prevent an uncaring landowner from cutting down all the trees around or in a nesting area.

Herons nest in colonial rookeries that are used year after year. Disturbance early in the nesting season can cause the birds to abandon a rookery, but the birds might come back if human activity decreases in following years. Working with landowners, several county governments and citizen groups in Puget Sound have begun to save heron rookeries. While trees are still being cut down throughout the region, attempts are being made to leave some protective buffers between new homes and heron nests. People are also trying to design developments creatively so that tall trees block the heron's view of houses and human activity. In general, buffers of about a thousand feet are needed to make this work. Access to these nesting areas should also be closed to humans during the nesting season, which begins roughly the first of April and ends by the first of August.

Since herons live throughout the United States, you have a good chance of watching these beautiful birds along streams, lakes, and ponds. Their needs in these habitats are similar to those in coastal forests. And their needs for clean water remain the same no matter where they live.

ONE EARTH

Rocky Coasts

Rocky shores rim many coastal islands and form a sharp line between land and sea along much of the Pacific and northern Atlantic shoreline. Starfish, urchins, snails, hermit crabs, tiny fish, and lush tangles of seaweed cover, crawl, or swim on and over the rocky beach. Steep cliffs give refuge to nesting seabirds. And big fish, including some of our most popular seafood species, swarm around the rocks when tidal waters are deep enough for them to swim.

Rocky coasts are among the most beautiful shorelines, offering people solitude, especially in places such as Maine's Acadia National Park and Washington's Olympic National Park. Both of these places give us a glimpse into the way life used to be along such shores. Sea otters, eagles, and whales feed offshore along the Olympic beaches; puffins, seals, and whales can be seen from seaside rocks at Acadia.

A FEW COASTAL TREES

With all the talk of disappearing shoreline forests, you may be tempted to begin a movement to replace trees along the coast. So, just what kind of trees should you plant if you had the chance to save a coastal forest or restore a damaged one? The following are some suggestions. But first try to save existing shoreline forests, and don't plant trees of any kind unless you determine they are suited for your area. Check a field guide or talk to a local nursery owner to make sure the trees you want to plant live in your area.

SPRUCE

Not all that long ago airplanes were made of a lightweight fabric stretched over a wooden frame, rather than of aluminum. As a matter of fact, the Boeing Aircraft Company, one of the largest airplane manufacturers in the world, started making airplanes in the Pacific Northwest in part because of the abundant Sitka spruce trees of coastal forests.

Spruce trees of any size are now very rare in coastal forests of the Puget Sound region. But big spruce trees can still be seen in places like the Olympic National Park coastal strip in Washington State. These ancient spruce trees grow as tall as football fields are long. The largest surviving Sitka spruce measures more than 20 feet around its trunk and is 305 feet tall.

COAST REDWOOD

The redwood depends on the sea, even though it can be found growing far from the ocean's roar. Now that the tallest Douglas fir trees have all been cut down by the forest industry, coast redwoods are the tallest trees in the world. They grow from southwest Oregon to central California, primarily in a narrow coastal strip that drips with fog rolling in from the sea. The fog runs into the trees and falls like rain. It is as if the trees could help themselves to a drink from the sky.

Some big redwoods are protected in parks. Others are being cut down — most of them, in fact. As you hold their tiny seeds in your hand, think of ways you might save them. Imagine starting a new coastal forest of redwoods from that tiny speck of life.

COTTONWOOD AND WILLOW

Most adults would probably think you were crazy if you told them you wanted to plant cottonwood trees. They usually don't like the little fluffy cotton that floats down with the tree's seeds. But what if you told them that planting cottonwood trees throughout the United States would help save the sea? A long time ago cottonwood trees grew along more rivers and streams than any other tree. They, along with willows and other *riparian* vegetation (plants growing along streams), were the trees that helped keep rivers from eroding their banks. But then they became the trees people cut down to make factories, docks, houses, and farm fields. Once they were cleared, factories were built, adding toxic wastes to the river, which wash down to the sea.

While it would be pretty difficult to talk people into moving factories away from the riverbank, it is not impossible to replace the many abandoned buildings along rivers with cottonwoods and willows, nor is it impossible to plant them along the thousands of miles of clearcut riverbank that exist today. No matter where you live, you could help the sea by replanting cottonwoods along streambanks. You could also connect cottonwoods from one place to another by getting in touch with schools downstream from your own. Get out a map. Trace a path to the sea. Start writing to kids in schools all the way to the coast. Maybe together you could create a trail of cottonwoods that leads straight to the ocean. Chances are good that a heron, an eagle, or an osprey will fly that same pathway from the sea to your own backyard.

Wherever rocky coasts form their strong lines at the sea's edge, sea life can be found and studied at great depths. Baby octopuses hide beneath rocks. Beautiful snails crawl over rocks while grazing seaweed that forms an almost continuous covering on many shores. Red and purple sea urchins seem to dance on spines that act as strong yet delicate legs, allowing them to move about on slippery stones.

Kelps and other seaweeds are *algae*—plants that do not have to spread roots in sand or need mud to grow. They receive nourishment from the surrounding sea, attaching themselves firmly to rocks with rootlike structures that usually keep them from being washed from the shore.

Like redwoods, spruce trees, and other land plants, sea plants are where animals hide, nest, and feed. Algae are the food base for chains, webs, and tangles of interconnected shrimp, fish, sharks, and whales. Rocks might hold all the pieces of the rugged coast together, but the plants are the soft nourishment that makes ocean life possible.

Rocky shores are usually very narrow and often steep. Wind and surf pound these shores, making life seem as tough for their inhabitants as it is on the meanest city streets. Life has become even more difficult along rocky shores because of oil spills, shoreline development, and other human activities. Declines of sea otters, puffins, and many other rocky-shore inhabitants reflect the changes brought to these beautiful coastal beaches by thoughtlessness. If you act to help these sea animals, maybe a better future for these rugged shores will be realized in your lifetime.

Sea Otters

Whiskered and fuzzy as a stuffed animal in a toy store, a sea otter will stare at you if you are at a safe distance. A large relative of the weasel and river otter, this sea mammal dives in Pacific Ocean waters to catch and feed on sea urchins, clams, fish, crabs, octopus, and other rocky-shore inhabitants. Sea otters sleep on mainland beaches if the shore is not crowded with people. Or they sleep out on quiet islands. Sometimes they even nap on the waves, wrapping themselves in kelp. Mother sea otters also hold tight to tangles of kelp plants while cradling their babies in their arms. Kelp keeps the otter still as the waves surge back and forth. The kelp also provides a rich feeding place.

Because it lives in cold ocean water, the sea otter has had to adapt to severe temperatures. It doesn't have blubber like a walrus or seal, but relies on its fur for insulation. The fur is so dense and soft, it is an effective barrier against the coldest winter seawater. But it is also very beautiful—one of the most precious and admired furs in all the world. In fact, the popularity of fur coats nearly brought these sea mammals to extinction at the end of the last century.

During the first decades of this century, there were only about two thousand sea otters in the entire world. Today sea otters have recovered slightly, but they remain threatened in Washington, Oregon, and California. Of these states, California has the largest sea otter population, but in central

---

SEA OTTER RELATIVES

Far more abundant than their larger relatives, river otters dive deep down into the sea to feed on ocean fish, clams, and crabs. They live along all of our coasts and inland, as well. Since they use both sea and land, river otters are unique indicators of the health of our coastal ecosystems. Their presence at a place where land, fresh water, and the sea come together means that many habitat features are healthy. If they are absent from such places, we should try to find which pieces of the otter habitat puzzle are missing. Sometimes the missing pieces affect our lives, too, since river otter food includes many of the same freshwater and seafood species we enjoy.

Sea otters do not and probably never did live along our Atlantic coast. But their relative the sea mink was known to swim along the shores of New England. That was before sea minks became extinct in 1890. We will never know how different the coast where they once lived might be today if they were still alive. Like the sea otter, the oceangoing mink must have played a key role in rocky-shore communities. There is no doubt that life along the New England coast has changed because of their loss.

At sea, marine plants are the food base. They come in many forms. Along the coast, most food for fish, birds, and even some whales is produced by salt marsh plants and algae, as well as by the highly productive seagrasses that grow in coastal shallows. Farther out at sea, most of the food is produced by phytoplankton, small sea plants that float freely, and by bacteria that also float around like other plankton. These bacteria cause some sea life to decompose, while providing a food source for others. All the small plants and plankton become part of complicated food webs like those that link phytoplankton to zooplankton (small animals such as the little shrimplike krill). The krill eat phytoplankton, and they, in turn, become food for much larger sea creatures, such as baleen whales, including blue, right, and humpback whales.

As on land, connections between ocean food webs are complex. Many ocean dwellers depend on both plankton and the nearshore marsh, as well as algal communities, for life support. Many ocean dwellers also receive nutrients and food from the land, especially those dependent on rivers for a part of their lives. Salmon, for example, depend on small streams, sometimes a thousand miles or more from the ocean, as well as the open sea. In the course of their lifetime they can eat mosquito and moth, shrimp and sculpin, herring and squid. During each step of their lives their food sources can be traced back to trees, marsh grasses, seagrasses, kelp and other algae, and the phytoplankton drifting on the open sea. When an orca whale then eats a salmon, how many land and sea plants — essentially, how many layers of life — are connected to its meal? And which ones are most important? The answer, of course, is all of them.

California otters face increased threats from fishing nets and from oil spills. Otter numbers have increased somewhat since gillnet fishing near California populations was restricted in 1982. But sea otters remain vulnerable to oil no matter where they live.

Sea otters constantly clean their fur, grooming the dense layer of insulation so that it can trap pockets of air. Like a down coat, these air pockets are a winter warmer. If oil spills wash against an otter, its fur becomes matted and the warm pocket of air disappears. Exposed to the cold, the otter is likely to die. More than a thousand sea otters lost their lives, for example, during the Exxon *Valdez* spill.

One reason large numbers of otters die during an oil spill is that they live in colonies. Spills along the Washington coast or along the central California coast could easily wipe out an entire population, since otters stay so close together.

To make sure otters are not seriously threatened by spills,

biologists have moved them to new locations, spreading the populations over wider areas. By 1990, San Nicolas Island in California had become the new home for 135 sea otters. But some of the transplanted otters had a different sense of their ideal home. Many swam away, letting the biologists know that sea otters prefer to choose their own homes. Or maybe they were trying to tell us that all coasts should be safe places to live.

Otters are also shot to death by people who believe that they eat too many crabs, abalone, or other seafood enjoyed by humans. Fishermen sometimes complain that the otters interfere with the human catch of valuable shellfish. But research has shown that all sea otters do not eat the same food. Some dine almost exclusively on crab, others on fish or shellfish. Some feed on entirely different foods each time they return to the same feeding area.

KELP FORESTS

Big brown seaweeds are called kelp. They grow in *intertidal zones* — places where the tide comes in and out — and in *subtidal zones* — shallow coastal waters never uncovered by the tides. Most kelps hook on to rocks with a holdfast, a rootlike structure. The growing parts of the plant include stems and leaflike blades that vary in shape from species to species. Two important kelps form forests beneath the sea, where lots of other kinds of seaweed also grow on rocks, on shells, and on the kelp plants themselves. Bull kelp will live in inland seas, while giant kelp grows mainly along the open ocean coast. Kelp plants are incredibly productive, growing as fast as four inches per day.

Like leaves in the highest tree branches, blades of kelp plants float on the water surface to form a kind of forest canopy. Beneath this protective layer of wide kelp blades, the long kelp stems act like tree trunks. These iridescent kelps shelter many animals in their dense tangle of soft stems. Within the kelp forest, fish of many kinds and colors hide from their predators or seek food for themselves. A listing of animals within the kelp forest would fill this book. Kelp inhabitants include greenling, black rockfish, sessile jellyfish, ribbon worms, limpets, sea slugs, scallops, porcelain crabs, many kinds of shrimp, kelp crabs, clam worms, brittle stars, urchins, abalone, herring, chinook salmon, clingfish, china rockfish, bocaccio, lingcod, wolfeels, harbor seals, sea otters, great blue herons, harlequin ducks, purple sandpipers, pigeon guillemots, marbled murrelets, and bald eagles.

Animals use kelp forests in many ways. Some feed here when they're young. Some cruise through briefly, and others remain their entire lives. People use the kelp forest, too, sometimes harvesting the plants directly, as they do trees on land. Kelp is used in many commercial products, but is far more valuable in the natural economy of the shore.

Clam-cracking otters dive deep down, scoop a clam from the seafloor, then swim to the surface with their catch. Many even bring a flat rock up from the depths, roll over on their backs, then smash the clam shell against the rock to open the tasty dinner. One of nature's few tool users, sea otters are highly intelligent creatures.

Otters not only dine within tangles of seaweed, they actually help the kelp forests grow. The lush, iridescent kelp forests are one of the most valuable coastal resource areas, and one of the world's most productive ecosystems. Individual plants grow as much as four inches each day and may reach more than 130 feet in length. Just as trees on land support plants and wildlife, dense stands of kelp support incredible numbers of other plants, fish, shellfish, and other sea animals. Baby fish seek shelter in kelp stems, seabirds rest on mats of kelp that float like tiny islands, herons use the kelp as a fishing platform, and dozens of marine animals eat kelp.

When kelp begins to grow, it attaches a rootlike base known as a *holdfast* to rocks or empty shells. Sea urchins graze the surface of these rocks and shells, mowing down the baby kelp plants. Wherever urchins are abundant, kelp forests are clearly absent. Wherever sea otters are present, the forest is saved. The otters munch the urchins, allowing kelp forests to grow back. Abalone, fish, and other seafoods valued by humans benefit from this otter-urchin-kelp balancing act. The balance effected by otters earns them the distinctive title of *keystone predator*. This prominent place in nature is reserved for animals that affect an entire community by their predatory behavior. Key to the entire rocky-coastal communities, the sea otter helps define what and who lives along the shore.

Oystercatchers

With daggerlike bills, oystercatchers pry open mussel shells or flip limpets from rocks to eat their soft interiors. On the

Pacific coast, black oystercatchers hunt along rocky shores. American oystercatchers feed in similar habitat on the Atlantic coast. But what makes both birds such good indicators of the health of the rocky-coast habitats is that they nest along the shore, too. Since they need safe places to lay their eggs and an abundance of food for themselves and their young, we know that wherever they are found in strong numbers, the habitat is healthy.

Early in this century, many shorebirds, including oyster-catchers, were hunted for food. Some, like the Eskimo curlew, were shot in such large numbers that they never recovered, even when hunting was finally banned. As is often the case, too little attention was paid to the decline of these animals before it was too late. Eskimo curlews are thought to be extinct. Fortunately, oystercatcher numbers increased after laws were passed to protect these birds. But they face new dangers today.

Dogs, cats, and lots of people now walk along shorelines where oystercatchers used to be able to nest. So they are found more often nesting out on remote islands. But even on islands, disturbances by people in boats or by people who come ashore to visit can cause an oystercatcher to flee its nest, leaving the nest free for a gull to swoop down and eat the oystercatcher's eggs or little ones.

Precariously placed just above where high tide lines form on the beach, oystercatcher nests are actually little more than dimples in the beach stones. Eggs sit among the rocks, and when storm winds push the ocean waves higher than normal, the oystercatcher can lose its nest to this natural cause of mortality. Also, when oil washes in from the sea, birds can lose their nest or nestlings to thick coats of petroleum.

Oystercatchers do not nest in colonies, as many birds of the ocean coast do. But they gather in flocks in winter. At this time of year, oystercatchers and many other shorebirds need clean and undisturbed beaches for feeding and for resting.

Puffins

Sometimes called parrots of the sea, puffins are one of the world's most beautiful birds. They seem to be wearing rainbows on their thick bills. They also seem to imitate penguins. Feathered in black and white, puffins are actually a lot like these distant southern relatives. Inhabitants of the northern Pacific and Atlantic waters, puffins use their wings to swim underwater. As if flying beneath the waves, they pursue a meal of fish.

When puffins take to the air, they look like flying footballs. Their stubby little bodies are best equipped for life in the water, and their short wings seem barely able to carry them through the air. But all of our puffins—the common of the Atlantic coast, and the tufted and horned puffins of the Pacific—manage to fly swiftly from one fishing area to another. When they dive, they are very well adapted to catching quick-swimming prey from swirling schools of herring, smelt, and anchovies.

HIGH ENERGY, HIGH PRODUCTIVITY

Stand in the ocean waves, and you can feel the water's energy. If you were a kelp plant called sea palm, your growth would be stimulated by that powerful force, that crashing energy of the waves.

Sea palms grow along rocky shores. They are pounded by strong waves, and the action of those waves brings them incredible amounts of nutrients from the sea. It also helps keep away competing marine plants not capable of growing in high-energy places, and provides protection from predators. These active waves literally knock the predators away from the growing plants. And grow productively is exactly what the sea palms do as a result!

Sea palms along rocky shores have been measured by scientists, who conclude that waves contribute far more energy to the growing plants than the sun. The plant growth per area of the sea palms is twice that of plant growth in tropical rain forests. This phenomenal growth has been compared to agricultural crop production. The wave energy is like the energy expended by a farmer using oil to produce high crop yields in a small area. Farmers drive tractors and other equipment fueled by oil that bring in extra nutrients by dispensing artificial fertilizers. They help keep competitors away by dispensing weed killers, and they protect against predators by applying pesticides and destroying natural habitat that supports crop or livestock enemies. But the big difference between the two is that plant growth on the rocky shores is fueled by wave energy, not by human interference with the natural economy of the shore.

FORESTED SHORELINES

Great blue heron

Coastal forest, Kenai Fjords National Park

Bald eagle

. Sea figs

Kelp forest

Big Sur. California coast

COASTS

Ruddy turnstones

Sea otter

Parakeet auklets

Oystercatchers

During their nesting season, you might see a puffin parent flying just above the waves, carrying a billful of silverfish draped neatly and securely in its mouth. Imagine how difficult it must be to swim underwater holding on to two or three slippery little fish. Not only can a puffin manage to hold on, but it can actually catch a couple more fish without losing the first ones caught, too!

Imagine also how tough it is for puffins to find a place to nest. They have had to limit their nesting to island shore-lines, since only islands give them a little protection from the crowds of people living along the ocean coast. Disturbance from dogs, cats, people, rats, foxes, and other mammals has led to losses, even on isolated islands.

Despite their name, common puffins nest these days within the United States only in Maine. They were killed for years by people who wanted puffin feathers for hats and by fish-ermen who thought these seabirds ate too many fish. Finally, at the turn of the century puffins were protected. Amazingly, this protection was not begun until their population had plummeted to an all-time low. Like survivors heading for the mythical ark, only two pairs of common puffins were thought to exist on our coast in 1900. By the 1930s there were about 20 pairs in Maine, and by 1960 about 100 pairs.

In one of the most creative wildlife recovery projects in history, the National Audubon Society began helping puffins during the 1970s. The project has successfully reestablished puffin nesting populations on new islands, in addition to the single location they had been returning to since 1900.

The efforts to attract puffins to the new nesting places took advantage of a technique once used only to kill birds. Decoys have been carved for centuries by hunters hoping to attract birds near enough to their gun sights to shoot them from the sky. Audubon puffin decoys placed on Eastern Egg Rock Island along the central coast of Maine work in the same way in that they attract birds to the island. But once the puffins land, they are left in peace, so the birds have started sticking around to nest. The small colony of puffins now residing on the island is there because of the puffin's curiosity and because people used their imaginations to help attract them to a new nesting place.

Also, recordings of puffin sounds have been used successfully on Eastern Egg Rock Island to help attract new nesting birds. Tape players have been installed near the decoys, offering a vocal as well as visual welcome for puffins that pass by. Apparently the puffin sounds have worked, since birds have been attracted to islands they had otherwise refused to visit, even when decoys had been placed at those locations. Now that new colonies are being established on formerly vacant islands, the hope is that puffin populations on islands in the north will gradually move south along our coast. For instance, if some of the 500 pairs of Canadian puffins now nesting on Machias Seal Island were to move south, then perhaps new colonies might also spring up on the many islands of Maine where there are no puffin nests now.

You can learn more about Atlantic seabirds by visiting their nesting colonies by boat. Contact the National Audubon Society directly to learn more about puffin-watching trips. Try also to make a puffin decoy of your own to attract more attention to the needs of these beautiful birds. Hold a puffin decoy contest, raising money to aid puffin recovery efforts in Maine.

You can also help puffins and other seabirds by telling your friends, family, and neighbors about the hazards of oil spills, fishing nets, illegal hunting, and other forms of ocean pollution that kill so many marine animals each year. The killing of an estimated one million seabirds yearly by monofilament drift nets could end immediately if changes were made in laws that regulate the fishing methods used on the open sea. But we will need more than laws against the use of these nets to prevent the overfishing that also affects other ocean life.

WHERE HAVE ALL THE PLOVERS GONE?

Piping plovers are delicately beautiful little birds. Their pale feathers are painted with the colors of their sandy world. This cryptic blending makes them hard to see along the beach. But they are also hard to see these days because they are losing the very homes to which they are so well adapted.

Coastal piping plovers nest along the Atlantic coast from South Carolina northward. But summer resorts along these shores have destroyed much of their breeding habitat. Used to long stretches of undisturbed sandy beach, they cannot adapt to these dramatic changes. They need isolation from human disturbance, isolation that is very rare these days.

In the past, piping plovers evolved a mechanism to deal with natural disturbance. Storms frequently pound the shoreline. Nests are swept away when high tide rises above normal levels or when rushed by storm winds. Sometimes gulls eat plover eggs. Raccoons might also raid a few nests. To deal with these losses, the plovers are one of the many ground-nesting birds capable of laying a second, third, and even fourth set of eggs.

While plovers can replace a nestful of eggs, they cannot replace their sandy beach habitat once a bulldozer has scraped it away. Only people's pleas for change can ensure the bulldozers don't take too much.

Studies of the Atlantic puffin in Newfoundland have shown that puffins raise fewer young when humans are fishing heavily in their waters than at other times. During these intervals puffin parents cannot catch enough fish to feed their babies. Out along the Pacific coast in recent years, tufted puffins have also failed to raise young ones. While no one knows for sure, this may be due to the effects global warming trends have had on fish populations there. Few studies have been done relating these immense changes to the individual lives of puffins or other animals. But we need to begin such studies now.

As many as 500,000 seabirds have died from oil spilled, dumped, or leaked into the North Sea and into the northern Atlantic along the coasts of Great Britain, Newfoundland, and the Baltic nations, where offshore drill sites are located.

This is about two times the number of birds killed during the Exxon *Valdez* oil spill in Alaska. It is also one of the main reasons people are concerned when offshore oil drilling is proposed along the coast of the United States. Watch the news for oil-leasing reports, and get involved in preventing oil drilling in your area if you want to help protect the puffins and other coastal creatures.

One relative of the puffin, the great auk, never recovered from the impact humans had on its life. Early-day settlers hunted the auk for meat and feathers. Once it was near extinction, people became fascinated by the auk because so few were left alive. Auks were shot and collected for museum exhibits. On June 4, 1844, the very last pair of great auks on Earth were killed. No decoys, no recordings, no amount of fund-raising will ever bring them back to the rocky coast.

ONE EARTH

Islands and Nesting Beaches

Seals, sea otters, sea lions, puffins, oystercatchers, gulls, terns, and lots of other marine mammals and birds used to be able to come up on the beach just about anywhere they wanted. They were safe to swim or fly ashore and hang out for a while, lay some eggs, or sleep in peace. Now virtually all our mainland shorelines are too busy for resting, nesting, breeding, or feeding.

Nesting beaches are rare on the shoreline, even in national parks and other protected beach areas. Islands offer the only true refuge for nesting birds of several species, and the islands where marine mammals can come ashore are precious places necessary to the survival of harbor seals, otters, and sea lions. Fortunately, many groups of islands have been set aside as wilderness areas. But all islands should be regarded as potential breeding grounds for the many marine animals that suffered when we took away thousands of miles of California, Florida, Texas, and other coastal beach shorelines. The following should give you some idea of how different species endured changes in their environment. If you live near the sea, maybe you can try to discover more about nesting birds and marine mammals. Maybe you could help some birds return to a nesting beach they used long ago.

Roseate Terns

Delicate on their wings, terns are like doves of the sea. The rarest of North American sea terns, the roseate has declined along the eastern shore north of Florida. Like other seabirds, terns were killed for feathers during the last century. Despite protection more than 75 years ago, they have not recovered. Today, the roseate tern is an endangered species.

Seabird scientists estimate that the total roseate tern population was 8,500 pairs in the 1930s. By the late 1970s there were only about 2,500 pairs. This serious rate of decline makes some scientists fear for the tern's continued survival in areas north of Florida. According to R.G.B. Brown and D. N. Nettleship, the rate of decline will lead to a complete loss of the roseate tern along our northeastern shores shortly after the year 2000.

Roseate terns nest on the European coastline of the Atlantic as well, where their numbers also are in decline. Along our northeastern shores, their vulnerability is due in part to the limited number of nesting places. Some 85 percent of the entire roseate tern population in this area nests within two colonies, one on Great Gull Island in Long Island Sound, and the other on Bird Island in Massachusetts.

One factor that contributes to declines in tern colonies involves a partnership we have in nature that many of us don't pay much attention to. But the numerous gulls of the world have been paying attention to us, and they appear to be the ones benefiting from human carelessness.

When people walk or drive a boat close to a tern nesting colony, the parent birds fly from their nests, leaving eggs or babies vulnerable to predators. Defenseless, the tern eggs and offspring are eaten by gulls.

Even the larger and more abundant common tern of the Atlantic coast suffers from gull predation. Although their numbers seem relatively high at present, common terns have also suffered population declines over the past several decades. Tern researchers consider the bird's populations highly threatened, as in New York, where careful attention is being paid to efforts that improve tern nesting habitat.

Protected from feather hunters in 1900, common terns numbered about 16,000 nesting pairs at the turn of the century. They recovered at first, climbing to a population peak of about 44,000 pairs in the 1940s. By the 1970s their numbers had crashed to fewer than 15,000 pairs. Their population increased again in the 1980s and is now declining rapidly from that high. In coastal Mississippi and Alabama the common tern is now extremely rare, totaling fewer than two dozen nesting pairs in both states.

To some people it would seem that the common tern is doing okay. There are still several thousand living on the Atlantic coast and more on the Pacific. But each nesting island must be thought of in the way we think of our own small towns and rural communities. Each island, just like each town, adds to the variety, diversity, complexity, and interest of life. Each is a little different from the next. Those differences are what help future tern populations survive.

We never know which small town in America will be the home of the next great basketball star, singer, scientist, gifted teacher, or architect. Likewise, the terns don't know which nesting site will produce the next generation of birds able to withstand environmental changes brought on by humans. Maybe the few terns left in Mississippi are the only ones with the genetic capability to survive a presently unknown pollution threat. Protecting that small group of birds, then, is as important as saving the dwindling colonies on our other shorelines. Evidence from other animal populations has also shown that each area has unique features; the terns of those islands are the only ones uniquely adapted to the regional habitat conditions.

You might help terns by reaching across the Atlantic to share ideas on how to save them, joining with European kids, since terns are some of the only birds that live on both sides of the ocean. Maybe you could be the originator of a Hands Across the Water project dedicated to saving all the seabirds of the Atlantic. If you live on the Pacific coast, maybe you could write to Japanese, Chinese, or Australian kids to search for ways to protect terns and other animals that share your common sea.

Look in a library with a good selection of bird books for THE ATLAS OF BRITISH BIRDLIFE by Bob Scott. This book tells you where you can write in Great Britain if you want to get in touch with other people helping seabirds. The book is also a neat model you can use to design your own book of seabirds.

OF MICE AND TERNS

In what seems an unlikely partnership, common terns on Great Gull Island, New York, are benefiting from a tiny mouse. Scientists introduced the grass-eating meadow mouse to the island, knowing that terns prefer to lay their eggs in fairly sandy places without a lot of dense vegetation. The mice have cleared small patches, nesting has increased, and the number of common terns on Great Gull Island has tripled in 10 years.

Encouraged by the success of common terns, field-workers on the island, an American Museum of Natural History field station, are now experimenting with habitat improvements they hope will help the critically endangered roseate tern.

To help with the efforts to save the roseate tern, researchers would appreciate funding donations, since monetary support from our government has dwindled. Send any amount you can to: RO-SEATE TERN FUND, American Museum of Natural History, Ornithology, Central Park West and 81st Street, New York, New York 10024-5192. Students 18 or older can volunteer to work on Great Gull Island in the summer, marking nests and banding birds for future identification.

To help further, write letters to your congressional representatives, urging support for endangered species funds. The roseate tern is in danger of extinction, and little or no money is available to help the birds remain alive in the future. This is true for many other vanishing species, and our government could be doing much more. Letters help, so write!

31

Brown Pelicans

Like bald eagles, osprey, and other fish-eating birds, the brown pelican suffers greatly when its prey becomes contaminated by pollution. Not many years ago, brown pelicans were very close to disappearing. That would probably surprise those of you lucky enough to walk the beaches or docks along many of our southern shores, because today brown pelicans seem

FROM YOUR BACKYARD TO THE SEA

The natural economy of the sea depends on rivers that wash into the ocean. In a way, this economy is like that of human markets. Exchanges are made between land and sea. You know about water cycles, about how the rain returns from the open sea, and about how some animals feed far out at sea and then return to streams to lay their eggs. Salmon do this. So do striped bass.

It has only been in recent years that we have been adding new twists to the natural exchanges, taking substantially from the ocean system. Lawn and garden chemicals contain toxins, many known to kill aquatic life. When we spread or spray them on the land, they also wash into streams, rivers, and the sea, where they affect hungry fish, seabirds, and marine mammals.

We also water our lawns and irrigate our farm fields with so much water that rivers actually run dry. Water once flowing into the sea is diverted to quench our thirst, as well. This interference with the natural flow of water has had major impacts.

Along the Colorado River, water is removed to sprinkle fields, to supply people in the arid Southwest with lawn water, and to provide drinking water in this rapidly developing area. Dramatic changes have taken place all along the river valley as a result. Since fresh water from this river is so important to the sea it once entered in greater volumes, the life of the Sea of Cortez has also been altered.

Fish such as the totoaba are endangered in part because the Colorado River water no longer enters the sea in historic quantities. Salt marsh habitat at the river mouth is no longer the same. Habitat upstream is also changed; miles of cottonwood forest that once lined the riverbanks are reduced to scattered remnants. Wildlife dependent on these streambank habitats vanishes. And an incredible 8 percent of the entire Colorado River's flow vanishes as evaporation into the skies above Lake Mead and Lake Powell, artificial impoundments behind two of the river's dams. That is enough water to supply the needs of 200 cities as large as Flagstaff, Arizona.

When you water your backyard lawn, you may not see habitat change as dramatically as the Colorado River communities affected by decreasing stream flows. But the process of change is the same, especially if your water supply comes from a river. You can help by trying to talk your parents into planting water-conserving lawn grasses such as buffalo grass. Native plants growing in your garden are also a good choice, since they are better adapted to the climate where you live. Chances are good they can get by on moisture that falls as rain.

so common and sit so close that many people pet them. These skilled divers seem as safe from extinction as human fishermen. But are they really safe?

Brown pelicans have partially recovered from the impact of certain types of pollution. When the deadly pesticide DDT was banned, most of the fish they preyed on were safe again, so brown pelicans returned. But populations in Louisiana and other areas are still threatened because of disturbance at their coastal nesting sites, destruction of nesting colonies, and the entrance of new pollutants into marine food webs.

In California an entire nesting population of pelicans failed to produce even a single baby bird because adults were feeding on DDT-contaminated fish. The source of the pollution was easily traced. A single factory that produced the DDT was contributing virtually all of the chemical that was killing the pelicans. If only the ocean's problems could be solved as easily. Finding new sources of chemicals that harm pelicans and other marine life is a difficult task, but the detective work of chemists and marine biologists may save future populations of pelicans if we tell politicians that's what we want.

Many new forms of pollutants enter the sea that we know very little about. We also don't know how they combine with other chemicals or what impacts they may have on the environment once combined. The effects of combined chemicals, called *cumulative effects* by scientists, were not even discussed when most of your teachers were college students. While few people have the training to even sort out the possible effects of these combinations, we all have the ability to think about how we are contributing to the deadly mixtures entering our sea. And we can all stop them from ever getting there in the first place.

Paint thinners, household cleaners, fingernail polish, boat paint, gasoline, lawn chemicals, and agricultural sprays all mix together as they find their way to our coasts. Sewage from boats and cities, acid rain, and wastes from nuclear

33

power plants pollute the sea, too. And industrial chemicals are dumped into landfills that leak into water sources swept out into the sea.

Alone, many of these chemicals can and do kill marine life. But when they accumulate, they are even more deadly. They may very well end up killing our entire sea.

We can help by refusing to use many of these chemicals. For example, the following garden products, used by millions of Americans to control insects, mites, fungus, or weeds, are all known to be toxic to birds or fish and other aquatic animals: Chlorpyrifos, Malathion, carbaryl, Carbofuran, Fenvalerate, Permethrin, nicotine sulphate, rotenone, sabadilla, pyrethrum, Diflubenzuron, Methoprene, Dicofol, Mancozeb, Captan, benomyl, Bordeaux mixture, 2,4-D, Glyphosate. Finding alternative ways to control garden and farm pests is a major challenge, and you can find out more about the problems and solutions by writing to the NATIONAL COALITION AGAINST THE MISUSE OF PESTICIDES, 530 Seventh Street SE, Washington, DC 20003.

You can also help by encouraging others to watch, learn, and respond to changes in life at the edge of the sea. Pelicans are great indicators. Like a flag, they wave their wings when all is well. Maybe you could write a new song, like an anthem, that stirs people's pride and encourages them to pay attention to changes in the life around them—changes that could signal danger for all the life dependent on the sea.

If you live near a pelican dock or a beach, you can also start a pelican count, watching other fish-eating birds, too. Keep track of their numbers and how well they do when they fish. How many times do they have to dive to catch a fish? By recording these kinds of observations, you will become more and more knowledgeable about your coastal area and can be a resource to others. If you live away from the coast, find the addresses of schools in several coastal cities or towns, and offer to be the census control center for all these schools.

As your field assistants at each school report their findings, you can compile the information so that each knows what is happening to pelican populations all over. Together, you can rally others to become more aware of the plight of the marine birds and mammals you love best.

Monk Seals

The entire state of Hawaii is a collection of nesting islands, some of the most beautiful in all the world. Stretching more than 1,500 miles, its string of islands and reefs are visited by many of the world's sea mammals. Humpback whales come here to give birth. Sea turtles feed along the rocky shores. Coral reef fish seem to bloom like flowers in the shallow waters. The islands are also home to many animals found nowhere else on earth, including the rare and endangered Hawaiian monk seal.

Monk seals once swam throughout the islands, but their populations were severely depleted by hunters until they were protected in 1909. Nearly a hundred years later, monk seals still have not fully recovered. Today, about 1,500 monk seals are thought to remain alive. That is as many as were brought

---

MONK SEAL RELATIVES

The Caribbean monk seal once swam in Florida Gulf waters. The last one vanished from the Earth's oceans in 1962, at a time when humans were first reaching for the moon and distant planets in satellites and starships launched from nearby Cape Canaveral.

Harbor seals, far more abundant than monk seals, inhabit the Atlantic and Pacific shores. They are common in many places but are critically threatened because of increasing levels of marine pollution. Harbor seals on the coast of Maine are thought to have the highest levels of pesticides in their bodies of any mammal in the United States. Those in Washington State waters have already shown the negative impacts of pesticide residues (the long-lasting chemical components that stick around in the food chain for many years after the deadly chemicals have been banned from use). Harbor seals in Puget Sound, Washington, have been born with birth defects, and others have been aborted, apparently because of the effects of pollutants.

into the port of Honolulu by a single ship during the height of the seal-killing days.

No one really knows how many monk seals there could potentially be, but we know why they fail to gain in numbers. Monk seals suffer from the very things that make the islands so inviting to people. A simple stroll on the beach by a vacationer who probably means no harm to native wildlife can frighen the seals, discouraging them from reestablishing themselves on beaches they once made home. Crowds of tourists, dogs, speeding boats, and tangles of fishing nets also displace or kill monk seals. For the most part the only places they can find for resting or for raising young are on the small, nontourist islands that lie to the northwest of the main islands we know best.

ONE EARTH

Open Sea

Far beyond the sight of land, the oceans wrap the Earth in a vast covering of salt water that once seemed to be a frontier as endless as outer space. We dumped our wastes into the sea as if the debris of our culture would somehow shrink from sight like the ships sailing away from our view. Syringes, plastic trash, oil, and dead whales washing ashore draw our attention to the dangers of these practices. We are connected to the open sea and will lose its life-giving force if we continue to abuse and misunderstand its needs.

Already, scientists have warned that the hole we have put in the upper layer of ozone in our atmosphere through our use of aerosol and other products is causing marine life losses. Dangerous radiation from sunlight unfiltered by the thin, protective layer of ozone has harmed food chains, especially in the Antarctic. But our actions have long affected the open sea, and perhaps no other group of animals more dramatically exemplifies that than the great whales, the largest living animals on our planet.

Temperature, salinity, food, breeding habitat — all these conditions and more affect where animals live in the ocean. We can look to whales to discover how temperature, for instance, influences the worldwide distribution of large marine animals. Smaller whales, such as dolphins, are found mainly in tropical waters, where they can keep warm. Polar seas may be too cold for smaller whales and for the kinds of food they eat.

By contrast, large whales, such as baleen whales, can be found in polar seas for part of the year. They are well adapted to cold water and are attracted to the enormous quantities of food found there, especially the vast soup bowls of krill. Krill are shrimplike animals. They may not grow to be more than two inches in length, but they are the richest feeding source for baleen whales. Krill reach their greatest numbers in a place known as the Antarctic convergence.

Here, subtropical waters flow into the cold seas of the south polar regions. When these waters come together, or converge, the heavier cold water sinks beneath the warm water. This churns up deep-sea nutrients. As these nutrients swirl to the surface of the sea, the tiny plants and animals that krill feed on blossom. Many coastal areas provide similar conditions of upwelling, creating rich concentrations of prey and predators. But none are as rich as the Antarctic waters.

Blue whales, right whales, penguins, seals, and other animals gather here to feast on the krill. But whales, like all animals, must also find the right habitat for giving birth and raising their young. Life is not just a bowl of krill. When the time of birth draws near, whales are known to make the longest journeys of any mammal just to find the right birthplace for their young.

Gray whales are among the best understood whale travelers. Their round-trip journey from rich feeding areas in northern polar waters to Baja California, where they give birth, is nearly 8,000 miles long!

Whales

Spinner dolphins. Tucuxi. Cochito. Beluga.

Humpback. Orca. Gray and blue.

Amazon, Benguela, Irrawaddy, Ganges dolphin, and narwhals.

Some of the names of these whales have a singsongy quality. If we could only understand their voices.

Whales are among the most intelligent members of the ocean community. Some are also the most musically inclined, the largest, and the most playful of all animals on Earth. Our recent attempts to save the whales is a great hope for the future. Unfortunately, that hope is dimmed by the realization that for some whales, our concern and action have come too late. If you could swim with the whales, you would visit almost every corner of the sea, and you might even learn how to save the oceans and coasts.

Blue Whales

Largest of all animals on land or sea, the blue whale probably numbered more than 200,000 individuals in southern oceans

WHALE WATERSHEDS

High in the Rocky Mountains, hundreds of miles from the sea, a sign marks a point at which the continent is divided. At one point, within Yellowstone National Park, you can look off to the south and east and see where land and stream eventually lead toward the Gulf of Mexico by way of the Missouri and Mississippi rivers. Look to the west, and all streams in this vicinity gather into the Snake and Columbia rivers and then into the Pacific. These two pathways to different seas encompass many millions of acres of land, many thousands of miles of stream. Imagine these vast chunks of America as enormous watersheds — an immense holding place that eventually carries water and all it brings from the land out into the home of orcas, humpbacks, and blue whales.

Shoshone Indians and others who have lived for centuries along the upper Snake and Columbia rivers understand this concept in a special way. Even though their ancestors lived hundreds of miles

from the sea, each year their lives were enhanced by the return of thousands of fish from the Pacific Ocean. Chinook, sockeye, and coho salmon, as well as steelhead trout, which grew to adulthood as far away as the eastern Pacific Ocean, not all that far from Japan, would swim back to lay their eggs in the upper Snake River of Idaho. These same fish of the Snake and Columbia rivers feed on squid, herring, shrimp, rockfish, and smelt out at sea. They are, in turn, the food of other fish, orca whales, seals, sea lions, and seabirds.

The Shoshone ascended the Snake River in years past to hunt in the highest points, above where salmon could swim. Here they hunted bighorn sheep, elk, deer, and the once vast herds of bison that lived within the same watershed as the salmon. The Shoshone also moved downstream to where they could catch fish swimming in from the sea. Now the Shoshone must fight especially hard to preserve the very few

salmon that are able to return to their streams.

Today watersheds such as the Snake and Columbia, as well as the Missouri, have been greatly altered, particularly by dams. Dams block migration. They also withhold so much water from the rivers that fish cannot return. Critical habitats are flooded. And water is released into the rivers at times other than those to which animals are adapted. But water still flows down to the sea from most rivers that are impounded by dams. Your actions can help make sure that water is clean. Doing this requires that the entire watershed remain healthy, so get to know the watersheds where you live. They might not be as vast as those of the Missouri, Snake and Columbia rivers. But we all live within a watershed that can probably use a little help so that harmful substances will not flow from the land, out to sea, and into the mouths of whales and other valued marine life.

alone prior to the days of commercial whaling. Today, there are fewer than 5,000 in that same region, and world numbers are thought to be about 6 percent of the total that existed before hunting began.

Full protection for the blue whale came in 1966. But we so completely altered the population that these whales are no longer the giants they used to be. Although they once grew to 100 feet or more, today a large blue whale will rarely measure 80 feet.

Where did the biggest whales go? Why didn't they regain their former size? More important, are there enough blue whales of any size left in the sea for their populations to survive into the future?

Think of a human town of 200,000 people being reduced almost overnight to a population of 5,000 with no regard for who stays or who leaves. Chances are good that a few of the people no longer living in that town might have been tall enough to play for the Lakers, the Celtics, or the Bulls. But it is rare to find a small town of 5,000 with the likes of the great Kareem Abdul-Jabbar, Larry Bird, or Michael Jordan. Variety in human populations is greater with increasing numbers. This is true in animal populations, too. No matter how much we eat or how much a blue whale eats, if it isn't in the cards for them to be long or fast, it just isn't going to be. They can't train to be these things. We can only hope the remaining whales have the survival traits needed to carry on during the long path to recovery hoped for by researchers such as Richard Sears.

Sears and other whale biologists have been studying blue whales for many years, learning to identify individuals, photographing them so others can also get to know one whale from another. As part of research being done in the Gulf of St. Lawrence and the St. Lawrence River, approximately 150 blue whales have been identified and named by researchers. Spindle, Hagar, and Crinkle can be identified by distinctive

More than 20 whale species have been observed in the rich island waters of the Sea of Cortez. Also known as the Gulf of California, this area is one of the world's most important whale habitats. Gray whales swim here all year long. Humpback, blue, and fin whales are also protected in the Sea of Cortez, where in earlier days they were nearly eliminated by harpoons shot from deck cannons.

Mexico has ensured the survival of many of the whales within the Sea of Cortez by protecting breeding lagoons such as those used by gray whales. Blue whales reproduce here, too. As in other waters, these blue whales are part of a breeding population that is unique to this geographic area. These breeding populations are relatively isolated from other whales and form what are known as *stocks*. A stock, like a tightly knit community of people, shares many characteristics of their species with others that live farther away. But they also have characteristics unlike those of the others. Stocks of whales, stocks of fish, and stocks of other animals are vital to the survival of the species; each group, or stock, contributes to the diversity that keeps the species healthy over time.

We may know very little about the specific features that vary from one stock of blue whales to the next, but we do know that particular stocks, such as those in the Sea of Cortez, are best able to survive in the waters where they have been found for many years. That is to say, even if blue whales were not an endangered species, the blues of the Sea of Cortez would survive best in the waters of Mexico.

Whale protection has led to successful ways of identifying and ultimately saving whale stocks, thanks to creative researchers at the University of Mexico. In 1980 they began keeping track of humpback whales by using the whale's "fingerprints" — unique and highly variable markings on their flukes.

Researchers include volunteers who come for the joy of discovery, as well as for the hope of helping the whales. They track individual whales moving away from Mexican waters into U.S. coastal areas using photos of their fluke markings. Those tracked include Humphrey, the whale that became famous when he wandered into the Sacramento River.

To date, more than 900 individual humpbacks have been photo-identified in Mexico. An additional 1,500 from Hawaii, 250 from California, and 500 from Alaska have given whale researchers a good view of how humpback whale population trends have changed since the banning of commercial whaling.

On the basis of the numbers of whales seen and identified, researchers estimate the humpback population in the inland waters of Mexico to be 1,500. Humpbacks are clearly recovering as a result of the ban on whale hunting. But the population is still only about 20 percent of what it used to be.

According to international agreement, a whale population is fully recovered when it reaches 60 percent of its former size. At that point, whaling nations will likely win approval to hunt the humpbacks once again. Some people believe that worldwide opposition to whale killing may not allow that to happen, especially since we are beginning to know whales as individuals. However, as this book was going to press, the Norwegian government announced that it would begin hunting minke whales in 1993, despite international disapproval of its plan. Unfortunately, no ban on whaling carries more than an agreement power; whaling nations can act on their own to hunt whales once again.

ISLANDS AND NESTING BEACHES

Kittiwake rookery

Common murres

Cormorants

Hawaiian monk seal

Male king eider

Horned puffins

California brown pelican

OPEN SEA

Humpback whale

Art Wolfe

Art Wolfe

Orca whale

Northern fur seals

Stellar sea lion

markings on their backs and tails, and by their color patterns. Pita, one of the most unusual blue whales, is one of the first to have been identified photographically. Pita is best known for being a fluker—a whale that raises its tail (flukes) just as it dives.

Identifying whales helps us know exactly how many exist in a given area, where they feed and raise their young, and what their migration paths are when they move from summer to winter feeding areas. Protecting and monitoring individual whales helps alert us to changes we might be able to do something about.

NEW HUNTERS OF WHALES

Hunting with a camera instead of a harpoon, whale researcher Jorge Urbana of the University of Baja California in Mexico photographed this humpback whale tail. Like our fingerprints, the distinctive markings on the whale's body identify it as an individual. Repeated sightings of this and other humpbacks will help Dr. Urbana and others understand more about the most important ocean habitats used by whales throughout the year.

Hunting with tape recorders, whale researchers in many parts of the ocean now listen closely to the voices of marine mammals. Already, individual whales have been identified by their distinctive voices. This adds to our ability to recognize the patterns of movement, breeding habitat requirements, and other needs of individuals. Just like you, whales appear to be a part of the crowd at times, while needing to have their own unique piece of the world at others.

Photo courtesy of Jorge Urbana

How long do individual whales live? What other animals do the whales spend time with? Where are the critical feeding places? As more and more whales are photographed and identified, and as more and more people get involved in helping and watching whales, researchers can answer these important questions. *You* can also help with this research in important ways.

You can adopt one of the individual whales in the St. Lawrence study through one of the most important and effective adoption programs of its kind. Contact the MINGAN ISLAND CETACEAN SOCIETY, 285 Green, St. Lambert, Quebec, Canada J4P 1T3. The society will send you a photo of your blue whale in return for your contribution. But that's not all you get for your donation. You also get to know that you helped to save valuable lives. Ask also about the chance

WHALE HUNTING

Even today whales are hunted in some waters. The bowhead or Greenland right whale has been hunted by Inuit whalers for centuries. They kill more than a hundred each year and are allowed to do so under current federal agreements, despite the concerns of many researchers that the continued hunting probably will mean extinction for the bowhead. Although the Inuit limit the number they kill, the bowhead whales will not be able to rebound from losses brought on in the past by non-Inuit hunters if the current killing continues. Until recently, European and American whalers slaughtered hundreds of thousands of whales. Our whaling industry changed whale populations dramatically. Our interference in the livelihood of the Inuit people also devastated their culture, a culture that had lived in harmony with whales for centuries.

To help whales survive and to improve the way we relate to native peoples whose lives depend on the sea, we can look to the example of the gray whale, which was saved from extinction.

Many coastal peoples, including the Makah, Nootka, and S'Klallam tribes of the Northwest coast, had, like Inuit hunters of the bowhead, killed these whales for centuries. When commercial hunters began hunting, the gray whales along the Pacific coast nearly disappeared. In 1937 all harvest of the gray whales ceased; today their numbers are very near what they were when only the Native Americans hunted them. Unlike Inuit hunters, however, the Makah, Nootka, and S'Klallam no longer kill gray whales. While they do still rely on the sea, they now harvest salmon, herring, crabs, and other seafood species, and many work as environmental biologists, too.

WHALE WATCHING ON YOUR OWN
In 1989 the total gray whale population was estimated to be 21,000 individuals. It is quite possible that anyone visiting the

to go out with the blue whale researchers on a whale expedition. Imagine helping the whales by traveling with them out on the open sea, learning their needs, and learning how to protect their ocean home.

Humpback Whales

Since 1985 a moratorium on commercial whale hunting has protected most humpbacks and their relatives. The International Whaling Commission has banned whaling, yet the practice continues because some countries grant themselves the right to hunt "for science," even though they sell the products of their hunts. Japan, Norway, and Iceland have also attempted to reopen the seas to whaling since the world closure was enacted.

Pacific coast today can see one swimming close to shore. Grays migrate up and down the western coast of North America and can be seen as they pass by many points of land. You will see grays just offshore at Cabrillo National Monument near San Diego, California, if you visit from December to February, when the whales move south to give birth in warm Mexican waters. Spring and summer are also good times to watch for the spouts of gray whales along Olympic National Park beaches, especially along U.S. Highway 101, where you can view Destruction Island, Washington, from a roadside pullout.

You can learn more about gray whales and one of the most social of all marine mammals, the orca whale, by joining a group of dedicated whale watchers in the San Juan Islands of Washington State. Write to the WHALE MUSEUM, P.O. Box 945, Friday Harbor, Washington 98250, to learn about the museum's Orca Adoption Program and other activities. Becoming involved with the Whale Museum will enable you to get to know Matia, Mozart, Sonar, Lummi, Oreo, Skagit, and dozens of other orca whales identified by whale researchers.

Imagine riding in a boat and seeing a sleek orca poke its head out of the water to watch you. Picture it leaping clear of the water's surface. That is exactly what you'll see if you visit in the summer. But you won't be seeing just an anonymous whale. This whale has a name and a personal history. For many active watchers, seeing Samish is like visiting a family friend — Samish is a mom orca that gave birth to her first calf, Capricorn, in the winter of 1986 at the age of 13. Her great-grandmother, which, like other members of orca families, swims with those it knows best, was still alive at that time. Orca families and acquaintances travel together. At times, groups are made up only of family members, including grandmothers, mothers, brothers, babies, aunts, and cousins. So maybe you should travel to the San Juan Islands to see her with your family, too.

SALINITY AND THE SIZE OF GREAT WHALES

Did you know salty seas help you float? Try it if you haven't had the chance — the ocean is an easier place to learn how to swim than a lake, river, or pool. This is because salt makes the water dense, holding you up in the same way it holds up fish and great whales.

Did you also know that we are more greatly affected by gravity on land than at sea? It's true, it's easier to fall down in thin air than in thick water. Because gravity's pull is modified by the dense water, falling down isn't a problem for ocean life. As a result of the extra buoyancy of salt water and of the gravitational differences, marine fish are larger than freshwater fish. Marine creatures in general are larger than their counterparts on land. This is true for crabs. It is true for mammals. In fact, the largest creatures to have ever evolved anywhere on Earth live in the sea.

The blue whale weighs two to three times more than any dinosaur that ever walked the Earth. Its tongue alone weighs as much as an elephant. A baby blue whale weighs six thousand pounds at birth and gains two hundred pounds every day of its first half year of life. This great size is possible only because the blue whale has adapted to the wonderfully buoyant sea.

Setting a different and more promising example for other coastal nations, Ecuador's president, Dr. Rodrigo Borja, has declared the 1990s to be a decade for ecological rather than exploitational development. His country (with a total population equal to that of New York City) has created the world's first complete whale sanctuary, banning all whaling within 200 miles of its coast, including the rich waters surrounding the Galápagos Islands, where humpback whales often swim.

Humpback whales have been a source of endless fascination because of their beautiful songs. Their voices are elegant reminders that we are not alone in our creative abilities. These songs vary greatly and change over time. Each is unique—no two whales have quite the same voice. That voice, like a fingerprint or a photograph, is now being used by whale researchers to identify individual whales in attempts to learn more about the animal's movements, needs, and behavior.

Humpback whales are also great travelers, spending summer months in cold waters at both poles. Winter months bring them to tropical seas around Hawaii and other warm-water areas, where they breed and give birth. Although increasing in number, they are no longer as abundant as they used to be. Before whaling began in the 1700s as many as 100,000 swam in southern seas, and 15,000 in the North Pacific and the Atlantic. Fewer than 10 percent of that number exist today.

Fur Seals

Many people think marine mammals or birds get entangled in plastic only once in a while. But this is not so. According to National Marine Mammal Laboratory scientists, plastic killed up to 40,000 seals each year during the 1970s.

Like our pet cats, seals are incredibly curious. They will often play with discarded pieces of plastic net or with packaging straps used to wrap shipping crates. But those straps and tangles of plastic, especially netting, can become deadly toys.

Sometimes a fur seal pup pokes its head through a plastic ring or net. As the pup grows, the plastic doesn't, and very often the seal is strangled. On the Pribilof Islands in the Bering Sea, Alaskan fur seals have been declining at an approximate rate of 5 percent each year. This decline led scientists to discover that plastic was causing the death of so many sea animals.

Except when they come ashore to breed and raise pups, fur seals are *pelagic*—meaning that they swim, feed, and sleep at sea. Although they can dive to depths greater than 400 feet, they often eat at night, when lots of fish travel up from the depths to feed near the surface. In the dark waters the seals may not have to dive so deep to catch dinner, but they do have to fear the nets and debris they can't see at night.

Foreign fishing boats stretch miles of plastic netting across the waves to harvest squid, salmon, and other sea animals. But the nets also trap seabirds and helpless seals. Every year an estimated 100,000 marine mammals of several kinds and possibly more than a million seabirds are killed in drift nets set by Japanese, Taiwanese, and other fishermen. Porpoises, puffins, albatross, and sea turtles die by the thousands in these nets. Many are never found, since miles of netting are often lost during storms or are cut free when they tangle.

Tuna

Like cheetahs on land, falcons in the air, and shooting stars across the distant sky, tunas travel with a swiftness matched by few other creatures in the world.

If the Olympics included a fast-fish event, the tuna would be a gold medalist many times over. Its body is designed for speed. Sleek and aquadynamic, the tuna's body tapers in a way that allows it to cut through the water efficiently. A thick band of muscle lines its vertebrae from head to tail. That dark band of tissue is adapted to help the tuna burst into speed and to maintain that swiftness for long distances. The muscle is packed with more oxygen-carrying capacity than the muscles of most other fish. With more available oxygen, the tuna does not tire easily.

Tuna fins are long and sleek, not wide and paddlelike. The body of a tuna is typically blue and silver, and tinged with reds or yellow. If we could see these beautiful fish in action, we could surely protect them from danger. Instead, we mainly place them in cans and spread them on bread.

Tuna and tuna relatives include about 50 species worldwide. From the consumer campaigns launched to help protect dolphins, you are probably well aware of the dangers tuna fishing poses for other species. But tuna fishing also endangers tuna themselves. Catches are declining, large tuna are not being caught as frequently as in the past, and scientists are beginning to issue warnings that tuna are in trouble.

In 1978 a maximum world catch of tuna reached 6.1 million tons. (This includes catches of mackerel and bonito, as well as tuna.) Fishing methods have become highly efficient, and many nations are involved in fishing fleets that search for tuna. In fact, tuna fishermen now use satellites and airplanes to find the fish.

Unfortunately, we have not designed methods to control and manage fishing as efficiently as we have created methods to catch fish. As one example of fishing efficiency, the Japanese have developed longline tuna gear. The longlines are just what they sound like—fishing line set with hooks and bait. Unlike normal fishing poles, the lines stretch for many miles. In fact, in one year the Japanese longliners set lines that, if strung together, could have circled the planet 500 times. Their more than 12 million nautical miles of line were set with more than 400 million hooks and caught 8 million pounds of tuna.

The Japanese and other longliners catch mainly bluefin

OZONE HOLE GROWS LARGER OVER ANTARCTICA

NASA scientists measure the ozone hole that has been broadening over Antarctica. The satellite they use is equipped to calculate the thickness of the ozone layer that encircles Earth in the stratosphere, shielding us from the sun's ultraviolet rays.

Measurements taken in fall 1991 were alarming. The ozone level had fallen to an all-time low of 110 Dobson Units, or just over one millimeter of ozone within a layer that is usually three times thicker.

The decrease in ozone is feared to have impacts on ocean life and is caused by our refusal to quickly ban the use of chlorofluorocarbons. CFCs are used in air conditioners and polystyrene (one cup made of polystyrene contains a mind-boggling 1,000,000,000,000,000,000 (a billion billion) molecules of chlorofluorocarbon). It takes more than 100 years for each of these molecules to break down, but only about 15 years to float up to the stratosphere (the ozone layer of the stratosphere is roughly 25 miles up in the air). Each CFC molecule can chomp down about 100,000 molecules of ozone. And

the layer gets thinner, and thinner, and thinner. . . .

Plans are in the works to ban CFCs by the year 2000. NASA scientists say that is not soon enough. Write to the president, other elected officials, and CFC manufacturers if you agree with our national space experts.

Who, other than people, will suffer from ozone depletion? Penguins, whales, seals, fish, seabirds, and many other animals that eat the krill that eat the plankton that disappear when the ozone layer grows thin. That's who!

BLUEFIN TUNA WORLD DISTRIBUTION

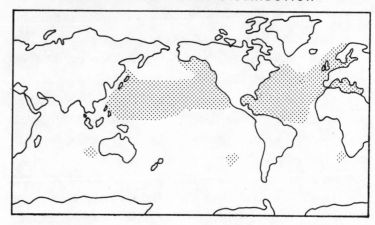

Bluefin tuna regularly move across oceans in what appear to be traditional migratory pathways. Like some other kinds of tuna, the bluefin lives in more than one ocean, but there are populations that are isolated from others, as you can see on the map of their worldwide distribution.*

The bluefin eats small fish like sardines, as well as mackerel and squid. It is the prey of sperm whales, orcas, great white sharks, and people.

* Note the isolated populations of bluefin tuna off the southwestern coasts of Australia, South America, and Africa (map locations based on information from the United Nations Food and Agriculture Organization). Unlike whales, tuna have not been studied thoroughly enough for the unique features of the isolated groups to be understood. Tagging studies have given us information on long-distance movements, but little is known about the ecology of the tuna.

tuna, highly prized for its delicate flavor. But take a close look at this magnificent fish. It should be prized for far more than its flavor. The bluefin is capable of swimming bursts of about 55 miles per hour. It can grow to 14 feet and weigh a ton. Imagine 2,000 pounds of fish sweeping and cutting the waves at speeds as fast as your car on the freeway. And the big tuna would outlast most American cars. It would, that is, if not so heavily fished. If left to live in peace, a tuna can live to be more than 30 years old.

In the 1960s an international organization was formed to begin the control of tuna fishing. But an individual bluefin tuna can be worth anywhere from $5,000 to $30,000, so pressure to keep fishing is great. Until recently, few people other than those who enjoy recreational tuna fishing have complained much about the decline of these incredible fish, even though populations in parts of the western Atlantic have declined to 90 percent of their 1970 levels. Within the last year, however, the National Audubon Society, the World Wildlife Federation, and the Center for Marine Conservation have launched a major effort to conserve bluefin tuna. Perhaps it is time for you to join their tuna-saving effort, too.

ONE EARTH

Coral Reefs

Coral reefs are the tropical forests of the sea. They contain a variety of life-forms in a dazzling display of color. But not all of the reef is alive. Most of it is made of nonliving material that tiny coral creatures produce as a shell around themselves.

Building a coral reef is a lot like a community project. Coral colonies—groups of living animals related to sea anemones and jellyfish—secrete skeletons of limestone that are used to hold the reef together. Other kinds of plants and animals, such as algae, also build upon these limestone structures. The coral reef is then covered by sponges, snails, algae, anemones, tube worms, and swarms of tiny marine invertebrates that are more or less the ants, spiders, and beetles of the sea. They, in turn, become food for larger sea creatures, such as moray eels, parrotfish, butterflyfish, angelfish, and sharks.

Sharks

Sharks are like the wolves of the sea. They are skilled hunters adapted to catching fish of many kinds. Like our wolves on land, many sharks are now in danger. Some may become extinct soon unless we get to know and care about them quickly.

ISLANDS AND EXTINCTIONS

The Hawaiian Islands are more isolated from land than any other island group on Earth. The uniqueness of these islands is in large part due to this isolation. Many plants and animals here, far removed from their relatives, have evolved into new species found nowhere else on Earth.

An estimated 1,700 plants grow on these islands and nowhere else. More than 200 of these *endemic* species — species that are unique to one particular place — are now extinct. Some 800 or more are endangered with extinction.

At least 68 of the islands' 86 species of land birds were unique to this area; 56 of these are now extinct.

More species have become extinct in Hawaii than in any other state, and these extinctions arose in many ways. Alien species — as deadly to the natives as if brought from another planet — push many plants and animals to extinction. As a dramatic example, about 4,600 alien plants now grow on the islands. Some of these quickly spread into the new growing areas, pushing out native plants. Habitat destruction kills more species, and others are either displaced by or preyed upon by rats, cats, dogs, and other animals brought to the islands by humans.

People also contribute directly to the disappearance of Hawaiian species when they shoot, catch, or otherwise exploit them so intensely that they become rare, endangered, and then extinct.

Sadly, the pathway to extinction on the islands is often quick, since island species cannot evolve defenses as rapidly as change occurs.

Beneath the waves, Hawaii's reefs and shores are home to about 450 kinds of fish. About 110 of them live only in Hawaiian waters. Some 18 percent of the algae are unique to the islands, and 20 percent of the mollusks, seastars, and brittlestars are endemic.

In the United States alone, several million pounds of shark are caught each year. This is well above the levels that shark populations can tolerate. Worldwide, the catch of sharks is about the same as that of tuna—more than 100 million individual sharks are caught each year. This number is rising fast, partly because we have depleted so many other fish populations.

Sharks haven't always enjoyed a good reputation, and people who catch them often do so in cruel ways. Fins are cut from sharks for soup. Still living, the helpless and mutilated fish are then tossed back into the sea. Regardless of the method used, the continued killing of sharks signals the beginning of a frightening sea disaster.

Like predators on land, and like the sea otter in kelp bed communities, many sharks are *keystones*. When they are removed from a reef or other habitat, the underwater world is changed. Sharks eat injured, weak, and sick fish, helping to prevent the spread of diseases. While we know little about the relationships between sharks and the rest of the sea world, we know enough to realize their absence is very hazardous to the places in which they live. As we learned from our treatment of whales, it does not take humans long to destroy large numbers of animals—too many for long-term survival.

The smallest sharks are just a few feet in length. Like the majority of its relatives, the largest, the whale shark, is not dangerous to humans. Whale sharks grow to 60 feet, but they feed on tiny plankton, just like the humpback, blue, and other baleen whales.

Fish-eating sharks are known to feed on herring, anchovy, pilchard, cod, crab, shrimp, salmon, other sharks, sculpin, perch, squid, mackerel, barracuda, flounder, midshipmen, lanternfish, halibut, saury, snails, octopus, hake, smelt, and many other species. This wide range of prey gives us an idea of how varied their diets can be. It also shows how much the shark is a part of every corner of the sea. Some sharks inhabit shallow reefs, others roam the open sea. Some exist in both kinds of habitat.

Great white sharks have given all the other members of the family a reputation for attacking almost any living thing.

TIDEPOOL MONITORING

If you live near the ocean, you can help save the seas by observing, recording, and monitoring the life you discover in quiet tidepools that form when the tide runs out each day.

It's kind of difficult to follow the path of a swift orca whale or to fly with the puffins. But you can help save their ocean home by keeping the smaller animals healthy.

Visit the tidepools. Record what you find, identifying animals and plants, too. Keep track of how they change through the year, and share your observations with others.

Adopt some tidepools and tidepool snails, limpets, and tiny fish.

Watch them carefully. Count them. Clean up their beach, too. Watch all the while for the spout of a whale or the wings of a puffin, knowing the bigger fish, the birds, and the whales, too, will all benefit from your efforts to keep their food supply healthy.

They do eat people and even attack small boats once in a while. Great whites spend most of their time near the surface, but they can dive to incredible depths, as far as 4,000 feet beneath the waves. They grow to more than 30 feet and can weigh as much as 14 tons.

Sharks are ancient sea creatures. They began swimming the world's oceans about 400 million years ago, long before there were any dinosaurs on Earth. With a skeleton of cartilage instead of solid bone, they have a sleek and flexible body. Their eyes are specially modified to help them see in darkness. Their skin is as rough as sandpaper. Even though their sense of smell is diluted in seawater, they are capable of detecting blood in the smallest concentrations. Their hearing is acute. They also have a unique electro-sensing system, which they rely on to detect prey. These sensors allow them to target and swim straight toward fish in distress.

Despite millions of years of continuous and successful adaptation to the sea, sharks may still disappear. You can help

STREAM MONITORING

If you live a distance from the coast, you can help save the sea by observing and monitoring life in rivers and streams. Look on a map to locate a stream near your home or school. Trace its path to the Atlantic, Pacific, or Gulf of Mexico.

All the land that washes into your stream eventually washes into the sea. And if chemicals or other pollutants wash off the land into the stream, they, too, will enter food chains that lead to the mouths of whales, fish, and seabirds. Animal life in your stream will also be affected by these ad-ditions to their environment. Stream insects are one of the first to show you that change is happening.

Adopt a section of stream, and get to know the surrounding land. With small mesh nets, or by turning rocks over with your hands, sample the insect life in your stream. The more variety of life, the healthier the stream. If you discovered only a few individuals or a few species, alert your fish and wildlife agency, asking the people there for advice and help in understanding your stream.

Because there are so many kinds of sharks, they can help us get to know many of the food, habitat, and community connections in the sea.

Basking sharks reach more than 40 feet in length, second only in size to the whale shark. They swim almost all the world's seas, opening their enormous mouths as they loop through the water in great circles as if to herd their plankton prey into a corral. Their mouths scoop in the plankton while their gill slits and gill rakers strain their tiny food.

Great white sharks grow to about 30 feet. They are thought to be migratory along many coasts, often following seals to islands where the marine mammals come ashore during the pupping season. Young great white sharks eat fish of many kinds, as well as crabs and other sharks. Adults eat large fish and marine mammals. Worldwide, great whites make about 50 attacks yearly on humans, usually in shallow water near beaches.

Leopard sharks live in the shallows, including reefs. Many leopard sharks are caught by commercial fishermen, an activity that threatens shark populations throughout the world.

Thresher sharks are predators. Their scientific name (*Alopias vulpinus*) means fox — from the Greek *alopos* and the latin *vulpes*. The thresher sometimes uses its long tail fin to stun prey. It most often feeds by herding small fish, such as herring, anchovies, or pilchard, into tight schools.

While only two to six babies are born in an average thresher shark litter, blue sharks have lots of babies. As many as 70 baby blues make up a single litter. They grow to an adult size of 12 feet, but have been reported up to 25 feet in length. They feed on pelagic fish, as well as those that live on the seafloor. Prey includes lanternfish, salmon, daggertooth, pomfret, saury, and squid.

Horn sharks grow to about three feet in length. They live around rocky reefs, feeding on crabs and small fish. Their young hatch from eggs that are encased in a strange-looking container resembling a hand grenade.

Pacific angel sharks look like skates and rays, with their flattened shape and wide angel-wing fins. As you might expect from their shape, they live on the seafloor. Their light coloration helps them blend into the sandy bottom, where they surprise prey that includes fish, squid, and crabs. Angel sharks have few young in a single litter, so the increase in shark fishing pressure on them threatens their populations. They simply cannot reproduce fast enough to keep up with the numbers being caught by commercial fisheries.

them survive by educating others about the more than 350 species of sharks that have never threatened and will never threaten our way of life. Most people, including the grocer who sells shark meat, do not know that not all sharks are dangerous.

Visit an aquarium to watch the beautiful zebra shark, the swell shark, or the gentle and shy epaulette shark. Then tell others what you have seen. Not long ago the world's whales were very poorly understood. Then concerned people like you became interested. As a result, most whales are protected by law today. Nations were brought together to study the situation and finally to stop the killing. Maybe you could be the first person to initiate an international project to help keep sharks alive.

THE DEPTHS

If you could follow a sperm whale as it dives into the ocean's depths, you would enter a section of the sea little understood by humans. The ocean depths are not covered at length in this book, mainly because they are so diverse, they would require books of their own to fully introduce you to their world.

The sea life you would encounter in the depths includes incredible fish with glowing lanterns that help them find one another and their prey. The dreamers, headlightfish, and lampfish all seem too much like creatures of the imagination to be real. But they, too, swim the sea. Such new and unusual species are being discovered within the ocean depths almost as often as new species are being found in tropical rain forests. Scientists, for instance, have discovered a very primitive shark, known as the frillshark, that is more like the sharks of 25 to 30 million years ago than it is like a modern-day shark. More recently, another new species, the megamouth shark, was captured by scientists for study. This 15-foot-long fish had evaded humans until about 10 years ago.

Even more surprisingly, scientists have been discovering entirely new habitats, such as "black smokers," or ocean vents, which are like chimneys that pop out of the ocean floor. Hidden within these habitats are even more new species that were unknown prior to the mid-1980s, including organisms capable of growing without the process of photosynthesis. Within this deep-sea world, life goes on without even so much as the basic life support of the sun. This habitat is like a self-contained system in which creatures live and die with no interaction with the wider world of the sea.

But ocean life in vents or other seafloor habitats is not the only new discovery awaiting your exploration. There are many more creatures, big and small, to be found. Perhaps you will be the one to lead the way to new discoveries. Maybe you will be the one to write the book on keeping the ocean depths safe from human invaders!

Coastal Wetlands and Soft Sandy Shores

No shoreline is more threatened today than coastal wetlands, those muddy, gooey, and marshy spots where the sea meets the land, and where plants, birds, fish, and mammals of both the ocean and the firm ground live. Once these creatures disappear, valuable links are broken and the ocean begins to follow a path of ecosystem destruction.

This disappearance is well under way from Alaska to California and from Maine to Texas. In San Francisco Bay alone, fewer than 15 percent of the marshlands remain. All up and down the Atlantic coast new homes are taking the place of these vital habitats. Presidents and governors proclaim that no more wetlands will be lost, then they allow developers to destroy the marshes as if they believed no one listened to their promises. But broken promises will mean broken futures.

At the edge of coastal marshlands there are almost always muddy beaches where you might lose your boots if you tried to walk beyond the edge of plant growth. But this mud is important for the survival of the plants and vital for the life of nearshore habitats. In fact, these marsh plants grow on the muddy beach, advancing slowly through the years onto the bare places. They move inch by inch as if marching into the sea by themselves.

The plants share these muddy beaches with shorebirds. Imagine your toes are so delicate, your body so fluffy and light, that you could run across the softest, muddiest beach. If you could do this, you would be just like tiny shorebirds. They run along these beaches in search of food. They eat lots of shrimp and shrimplike animals. Many kinds live in coastal wetlands and muddy beaches, and pretending to be one of them is a great way to get to know shorebirds and their needs.

All too often, the marsh and the mudflats at its edge are cut off by seawalls, piers, docks, or other construction. Filled, excavated, and destroyed, the marshes sink from existence, and along with them go tons of food needed by salmon, striped bass, seals, whales, and thousands of seabirds. On one square foot of beach there can be more than 9,000 individual organisms—mainly worms, crustaceans, and polychaetes—so imagine how much life is lost when a thou-

SHOREBIRDS

Shorebirds include some of the most visible and most diverse animals of the coast. They fly singly or in enormous flocks, visiting many kinds of beaches, from rocky to muddy shores. Each type of shorebird feeds on slightly different kinds of food, selecting prey by using a bill designed just for feeding at certain depths in sand or water, or for picking prey from a special habitat.

Curlews and godwits both have long bills, but the curlew's curves down and the godwit's upward. Both can feed in water as deep as 8 or 10 inches, snatching food from the sandy bottom. They can also probe in beach sand or mud to a depth of about 6 or 7 inches. But the tiny least sandpiper can probe only to a depth of about an inch with its short, narrow bill. Western sandpipers, dunlin, sanderlings, knots, sharp-tailed sandpipers, yellowlegs, dowitchers, stilt sandpipers, willets, tattlers, and white-rumped sandpipers all pick at the sand surface or feed at depths in between.

Some sandpipers fly together in large flocks. Others select more isolated shores and feed more or less alone or in small groups. This is especially true of sandpipers adapted to rocky shores. Purple sandpipers, rock sandpipers, and turnstones usually fly in small flocks because their habitat, wavewashed and kelp-covered rocky shores, is a very narrow band that stretches along the ocean coast. Sandpipers that travel in flocks of several hundred birds typically seek their food on the broad, expansive shores that stretch for many miles along the coast in much wider bands of sand.

No matter where they feed, shorebirds are important food for birds of prey, including the rare peregrine falcon. Winter flocks of sandpipers gather together to form groups of several thousand birds. They are joined by flocks from rocky shores, gathering in muddy beach flats that line quiet bays and estuaries protected from severe winter storms. Here they become a link in marine food chains that provide an example of a quick transfer of energy from marine plants to the animal world. And they offer an example of a transfer of energy from one of the ocean's most abundant life forms to one of its rarest.

Tiny shrimp and shrimplike animals feeding on marine algae are picked from the surface of the beach by energetic flocks of sandpipers. As shorebirds fly up from one feeding place to another, peregrine falcons dive into their midst, snatching birds from the flocks. The rare falcon is nourished. Individual sandpipers are seemingly not missed from the crowded flocks. The many millions of tiny shrimp and tons of marine algae supporting the shorebirds continue to grow and multiply. Life goes on as long as the chain from plant to shorebird to falcon is not disturbed.

Humans continually destroy animals at the top of the food chain. Falcons are rare in part because years ago they lost nesting habitat. But they became rare primarily because the food chain was contaminated by pesticides washing down rivers and into the sea, where algae, shrimp, shorebirds, and, eventually, falcons ate the wastes of human agricultural spraying. But as you can see, they are needed to keep the shoreline's natural economy balanced.

CORAL REEFS

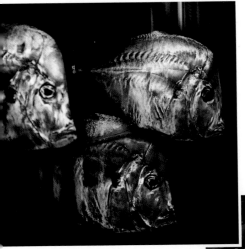

Lookdowns

Lionfish

Sea anemone

Starfishes

Leopard shark

COASTAL WETLANDS

Willet

Marbled godwits

Sanderlings

Atlantic ridley turtle

American crocodile

Hawksbill sea turtle

Manatee

Jellyfish

Sally Lightfoot crab

Ghost crab

Silver-spotted sculpin

sand acres of muddy shoreline is destroyed. Just try to do the math.

Read SAVE OUR WETLANDS, soon to be published in this Audubon series, and check out a couple of books about life in muddy and sandy beaches, especially ones giving you lots of identification clues to the smaller animals living on the beach itself. Then look up what some of the larger fish, birds, and other marine animals like to eat. Try to help others understand how complex marine food webs can be and how disastrous it is to lose any more of our coastal wetlands. If you happen to get elected to the presidency someday, you could even make a promise to save the wetlands. But you have to promise to keep your promise.

Sea Turtles

To lay their eggs in the sand, sea turtles must come ashore. Mother turtles bury soft-skinned eggs before they swim back out to sea. Eventually, the eggs hatch and the tiny turtle babies wiggle through the sand and scurry into the surf. Before they return to lay their own eggs, the young turtles will live at sea, eating a wide variety of sea creatures or sea plants. But many threats prevent them from ever returning to those nesting beaches.

Your commitment is urgently needed to help most of the world's sea turtles. The olive ridley sea turtle is one of the most widespread. It nests on islands, but more commonly on mainland shores, sometimes in incredible numbers. As many as 100,000 or more female olive ridleys are known to have come ashore in what are among the most spectacular mass gatherings of a single animal species. Although sea turtles do nest on U.S. shorelines, these mass gatherings are now restricted to other coastal countries where habitat is more thoroughly protected. Large nesting populations of the olive ridleys can be seen on the Pacific coast of Mexico and in Costa Rica.

Olive ridleys can dive to depths below 400 feet and remain underwater for long periods, thanks to lungs that are adapted to a seagoing lifestyle. They do not have to drink fresh water; their food and salt water satisfy their thirst. They feed on shrimp, crabs, snails, squid, and fish eggs. Though numerous, they may actually be the most threatened sea turtle. Because they mass together in such large numbers during nesting time, they are highly vulnerable to overhunting at these single locations. Hunted for their crocodilelike skin, olive ridley sea turtles have been killed in numbers that have reached more than 100,000 each year.

Kemp's ridley sea turtles frequent the Gulf of Mexico and the Atlantic coast of North America, entering Chesapeake Bay, an important summer feeding area. Here they feed on blue crabs after migrating up the coast. On their migratory journey, the turtles are killed in such large numbers that they are thought to be in danger of extinction. They often drown in shrimp trawling nets. Many turtles and other nonshrimp creatures are caught in these nets, only to be thrown overboard after they are found dead.

A new requirement called a TED, or turtle excluder device, has helped save turtles from being caught in the nets. The National Marine Fisheries Service enforces use of the TEDs, and research since the 1990 requirement went into effect suggests that the devices work. Turtles are not being killed in such large numbers. We must hope that it is not too late. That hope grows stronger with such efforts as the sea turtle recovery program initiated by scientists and volunteers on Padre Island in Texas.

Turtle savers on Padre Island established a new nesting area by gathering eggs from what had been the very last nest site in the world for the Kemp's ridley and transporting them to the new site. Until the 1950s, as many as 40,000 females came ashore all on one beach near the Mexican village of Rancho Nuevo. Today fewer than a thousand nest on this beach. But scientists believe that with a new site in Texas and with protection from shrimp fishermen, the Kemp's ridley may be saved. This sea turtle will remain safe, though, only with help from people patrolling its nesting beaches.

Leatherback sea turtles are the largest turtles and the greatest travelers. They are named for their soft, leathery *carapace*—the top part of their shell. Nesting now occurs along the tropical beaches of Mexico, Costa Rica, and South America, where deep water hugs the shore. Because their shell is soft, they tend to avoid rocky shallows and coral reefs. But outside the nesting season they will swim great distances and approach some rocky shores as far north as Canada and Norway.

Leatherback turtles love to eat jellyfish, a habit that didn't cause them much grief until Americans went plastic crazy during the 1960s. Everybody thinks life would not be possible without plastic. But for leatherbacks, life would not be possible without jellyfish. Unfortunately, jellyfish look a lot like plastic bags. Slippery, slimy jellyfish are eaten by leatherbacks with their scissorlike, deeply notched jaws. But these turtles' jaws

JELLYFISH

Relatives of sea anemones and coral, the jellyfish eaten by sea turtles float in the world's oceans, sometimes in dense masses you might see along the shore. Their transparent bodies are radially symmetrical, like a basketball or an orange. They can be perfectly round, but lots of jellyfish are shaped like your cupped hand. If your hand were a jellyfish, delicate filaments would trail down from your palm. On the real thing, these tentacles carry tiny toxic stingers that help jellyfish capture their prey.

Jellyfish are carnivores, some feeding on planktonic lobster larvae. In fact, they are such efficient lobster predators that jellyfish population peaks are usually followed by poor lobster population growth periods. People who have fished in the sea for many years will tell you that fish may even move away from large concentrations of jellyfish. But the leatherback turtle moves into these areas to feed on its favorite food.

Some people also eat jellyfish, mainly after it is dried, sliced, and seasoned with a little soy sauce, garlic, and sesame oil. But all jellyfish are toxic to a certain degree. So most jellyfish consumers pull away the tentacles. The leatherback turtle, however, has adapted to eat jellyfish, tentacles and all.

apparently lack sensitive taste and touch, because they can't tell the difference between jellyfish and plastic bags. They swallow the bags we throw away by the millions. When swallowed, these plastic bags can and do kill thousands of leatherback turtles.

A famous dish, green turtle soup, is named for Pacific green turtles. The thick, green, jellylike base for the soup is found only beneath the shell of a green sea turtle, and this has caused many problems for the survival of this sea reptile. Even though green turtles are threatened by overhunting, marine pollution, egg snatching by hungry prey, habitat destruction, and fishnet entanglement, they continue to be killed for the soup stock. Amazingly, widely published cookbooks still include recipes for turtle soup without even mentioning the dangers facing the main ingredient.

Named for its narrow head and pointed beak, the hawksbill turtle rarely swims beyond tropical waters. Of all the different turtles, this one is the closest to extinction because of demand for tortoiseshell. Eyeglasses, combs, hair clips, and many other products cause the death of most hawksbills, or careys, as they are called in Latin American countries.

The most significant and destructive demands for turtle shells come from the Japanese, Italian, and German markets. For example, the Japanese revere turtles as a symbol of longevity. Because of this ancient belief, baby turtles are killed, stuffed, and sold to Japanese people, who place the turtle trophies on their walls in the hope that this practice will lead to longer lives. But as many as 100,000 baby turtles die each year to keep this custom alive. India, the Philippines, and Indonesia are the major exporters of the hawksbills.

Raw turtle shell imported to Japan has accounted for about 90 percent of the total world supply of hawksbill carapace. Fortunately, as this book was going to press, Japan agreed to phase out imports of hawksbill turtle shells. Watch for updates on how this important decision affects turtles worldwide.

Sea turtles have survived on Earth for about 150 million years. Because of human greed, six of the seven sea turtle species are listed as endangered or threatened and have been given protection by our government under laws such as the Endangered Species Act and the Convention on International Trade in Endangered Species. CITES is an agreement between nations that helps prevent destructive import and trade of endangered species. It is the same agreement that helps protect rhinos, elephants, and leopards. Even with these laws, however, there is not enough protection extended to save the turtles. Sea turtles will be fully protected only when people voice their concern clearly and often.

Maybe you could help save the world's sea turtles by starting a campaign to protect them in countries where such concern has not yet been expressed. Learn more about sea turtles and efforts to save them by contacting the VIRGINIA MARINE SCIENCE MUSEUM, 717 General Booth Boulevard, Virginia Beach, Virginia 23451. Also, read more about turtles in books such as those by Archie Carr, the one man who has done more than any other to call attention to their plight. His books include THE WINDWARD ROAD, published by Florida State University Press in 1979. And write to the MASSA-CHUSETTS AUDUBON SOCIETY, Natural History Travel, Lincoln, Massachusetts 01773, to find out about turtle research projects you can join in Costa Rica.

Manatees

Swimming in the warm coastal waters of Florida, the manatee seems to live in paradise. This gentle sea mammal grows to an enormous size; its dark gray to black body can be nearly 15 feet long and weigh almost a ton. It feeds on water plants and seaweeds that grow in coastal rivers and shallows.

Like people and wolves, manatees spend a lot of time together. The social manatees greet one another with flipper hugs and muzzle kisses. They also communicate with one another through a language that includes sounds somewhat like those of whales. Some sounds are even like those a person might make, such as their shrill scream when frightened.

Female manatees warn their young ones of danger with an alarm call and keep their babies with them for at least two years. The baby manatee is born underwater, but the air-breathing sea mother brings the little one to the surface quickly, swimming with the newborn on its back. Little by little, the baby manatee is brought back down beneath the surface, where it is nursed for the first year or a little longer.

American manatees have been hunted in the past for food. Today populations are severely reduced in number. They were once widespread throughout coastal lakes, rivers, and marine shores from the southeastern United States to at least as far south as the Amazon River.

The Amazon manatee was almost driven to extinction during the days when it was killed for oil, skin, and food. As many as ten thousand Amazon manatees were killed each year up to the late 1950s. Finally, in 1973 the Brazilian government protected them, but few remain alive today.

Larger numbers of manatees remain along the west coast of Africa. But the related dugong has suffered greatly. It is now gone from the Mediterranean Sea and declining throughout its range, except in Australia. At one time it also ranged from southeastern Africa to the coast of China, north almost to Japan. Like the manatee, the dugong is killed by boats, nets, and people who hunt these sea mammals.

A manatee eats as much as one hundred pounds of aquatic plants each day, nibbling with its lips and grasping plants with its flippers. Like plant eaters on land, manatees affect plant communities, helping to define the structure of the water world. Like enormous weed eaters, the manatees even clear paths along rivers where people like to travel by boat. Open water areas are created as the manatees feed; where manatees are absent, plants such as water hyacinth can choke the waterways. Ironically, the same boats that benefit from manatee clearing often strike and kill the grazing sea creatures.

Studies in Florida signal a frightening coastal warning to all of us, and the manatees are the first to show signs that all is not well beneath the sea. More and more boats are crowding Florida coastal waters, adding oil pollution to shorelines and shallow waters, while disturbing natural balances, especially among manatee families.

More than 1,000 manatees were found dead in Florida waters during the 1980s. The number dying each year increases, with most casualties being caused by boats' hitting manatees. When an adult female manatee dies, her baby usually dies, too, since the mother is no longer able to care for her young one. Injured females are also less likely to be able to care for their young, adding to infant mortality rates.

As more and more manatees die each year, more and more boats are added to the coastal fleet. The number of boats registered in Florida waters is now close to a million. Probably more troubling for the manatee, the boats are traveling faster each year. Many boats travel at speeds of 60 miles per hour, some exceeding 100. At such speeds it is almost impossible to avoid hitting a manatee as it peacefully swims just beneath the surface. Virtually all adult manatees wear some scar resulting from being hit by a boat at some time in their lives, lives that seem to grow more precarious as human activity grows faster and faster.

You can join others in helping the manatee by contacting the SAVE THE MANATEE CLUB, 500 North Maitland Avenue, Suite 210, Maitland, Florida 32751.

Crocodiles

More than 70 million years ago, the great age of the reptiles came to an end. Almost.

Most of the dinosaurs became extinct, vanishing for all

CASE STUDY: A COASTAL AREA SAVED

Bowerman Basin is a shallow, muddy coastal area in Washington State within Grays Harbor and not far from the town of Aberdeen. When a small group of people learned of plans to fill, dredge, and destroy the mudflats, they adopted Bowerman Basin as if it were their own backyard, their own home. They loved the birds that used the area, enjoyed hiking and exploring the beaches, and cared enough about their community to get together to try to save the beach from what seemed to be imminent destruction. A group called the Friends of Bowerman Basin was formed.

They called and wrote to their representatives in Congress. They worked with state officials in wildlife agencies and state legislatures. They enlisted help from the National Audubon Society, speaking and writing about their cause at public meetings, and in newspapers and magazines. Fund-raisers helped obtain donations to pay for educational efforts. With only a few hundred dollars and the efforts of a small group of people, Bowerman Basin became a national wildlife refuge.

Janet Anthony was largely responsible for protecting Bowerman Basin and its thousands of shorebirds, rich feeding grounds for fish, and vital habitat for the endangered peregrine falcon. Janet was a student when she first became interested in helping the birds of the area. She visited the marshes and mudflats and started to plan ways to ensure their safety. She was the person who organized the Friends of Bowerman Basin, hoping to educate others about the values of the area. But she also created a fun way to help celebrate Bowerman Basin by organizing the Festival of Shorebirds. The festival was held each year from 1983 to 1988 in a mall where a large audience was assured.

Audubon and other environmental groups attended the festival, setting up booths to help people learn about mudflats, shorebirds, falcons, and other important features of the basin ecosystem. As a part of Grays Harbor, the mudflats produce tremendous numbers of tiny animals, especially the shrimplike corophium, a food source for dozens of larger animals. Since salmon and other valuable seafood species enjoyed by people also depend on corophium for their food, the people of Grays Harbor also learned a lot about how important Bowerman Basin is for their own livelihood. This is especially true in Grays Harbor, where many people are commercial fishermen or enjoy fishing for fun.

Janet Anthony and the Friends of Bowerman Basin recognized that this ecosystem was connected to people's lives in many ways. At her festivals Janet gained support from many people with a wide range of interests.

Backed by their support, Janet took trips to Washington, DC, where she learned to work with Congress at workshops sponsored by the National Audubon Society. She visited congressional representatives and met with officials of the U.S. Fish and Wildlife Service, the agency responsible for managing the thousands of shorebirds that visit Bowerman Basin and other such basins each year.

She began to lobby everyone she met, interesting them in the idea of founding a wildlife refuge at Bowerman Basin. But while she was gone, commercial developers were trying their best to interest state officials in filling up the mudflats to construct a racetrack. The Friends of Bowerman Basin were nearly defeated. Commercial development permits were issued by Hoquiam, a city on Grays Harbor, and by the Washington State Department of Ecology, an agency supposedly responsible for protecting the shorelines.

But in 1985 Janet Anthony and the Friends of Bowerman Basin sued the city of Hoquiam and the ecology department. The Friends lost the suit, but the lengthy court case and changes in the issuance of permits for filling ultimately prohibited the commercial developer's plans; success came without official victory.

Support from Audubon and other environmental groups, combined with citizen interest and the testimony of state and federal wildlife biologists, finally resulted in the establishment of a refuge at the site. Today final stages of refuge planning are under way. Although this seems like a happy ending, can we be sure that Bowerman Basin and its wildlife will always be safe? Will it always be protected because it is a wildlife refuge? The answer lies in one concept, one idea, that is at the core of understanding how we can save our oceans and coasts. Bowerman Basin, like all coastal areas, is part of a larger ecosystem. It is not an isolated place. It is connected to all of Grays Harbor and all of the Pacific Ocean. Ecological connections tie the mudflats, the shorebirds, and all inhabitants together in ways that cannot be protected simply by drawing a line on a map and calling a place a refuge.

As a wildlife refuge, the immediate area within the boundaries is protected from filling, dredging, and commercial development. But the boundary lines were drawn quite small. Critical mudflat areas were left out of the official refuge area. Biologists now fear that these areas may be filled as development proceeds in Grays Harbor. An airport located on the edge of the shoreline, as many in

American coastal cities happen to be, may be expanded by filling the mudflats surrounding the refuge.

People who want more airport runways have lots of money to spend building them. People like Janet Anthony and the Friends of Bowerman Basin have few funds and little time to fight the battles that continue to arise.

People like Janet deserve our thanks for having done such a tremendous job in creating the refuge. They worked hard to create a place where shorebirds and falcons can be safe. But environmental victories are always short-lived. New threats always arise, such as the airport.

To truly protect ecosystems like Grays Harbor and Bowerman Basin, we need to think of them as enormous homes that extend beyond the fences we build around them. The mudflats are like grocery stores that serve those homes. At the shoreline edge, salt marsh wetlands offer a place for birds to rest when tidal waters flood in over the mudflats. The marsh also produces food and shelter for many animals and helps protect uplands from flooding. The tidal waters flow in to mix each corner of the inland sea of Grays Harbor with every other corner. Salmon, otters, falcons, flounder, ducks, geese, oysters, and enormous gray whales all de-

pend on the ecosystem to work in harmony. Each piece of the puzzle that is Grays Harbor needs to work, to function.

The mudflats of Bowerman Basin work best when they have lots of tidal water flowing in and out each day. If these valuable tidal flats are filled and the tidal water is prevented from flowing, then the shorebirds, the salmon, and eventually the people of Grays Harbor will begin to disappear.

No matter where you live, you can help Bowerman Basin and other coastal ecosystems the way Janet Anthony and the Friends of Bowerman Basin did. Adopt a beach or a river that flows to the sea. Select an indicator animal to protect along your shoreline or riverbank. Begin to promote your own Friends of the Sciota River, Kennebec River, Delaware Bay, Tampa Bay, Humboldt Bay, Great Bay, or Mississippi River. Go to a local mall and ask if you can hold your own Great Blue Heron Festival, Turtle Day, Trout Rally, Darter Day, or even another Shorebird Festival. Attend meetings of your local Audubon Society. Keep an eye on local development, and support creation of parks or refuges. It takes only one person to start what may become a national interest in your own special place of concern. You *can* save the sea and its inhabitants.

time except as fossil reminders of that time in Earth's history when apatosaurs, pterosaurs, and tyrannosaurs roamed the land. Only two members of this reptile group have survived into our time, alligators and crocodiles.

Crocodiles still live in North America, but the American crocodile, like its dinosaur relatives, is threatened with extinction. Demand for its thick and beautiful skin has not helped it persist in a world that is also losing coastal wetlands—the crocodile's habitat—at a rapid rate.

Crocodiles have lived on Earth for more than a hundred million years. If they kept family scrapbooks, we could look back to a time long before we first appeared. How many changes in the coasts would the crocodile photo album portray? What could we learn from those natural changes of the past?

On the Pacific and Atlantic coasts, crocodiles inhabit shorelines from Mexico to northern South America. Within the United States, crocodiles now live only in Florida. They are almost entirely restricted to seawater areas, ranging from Biscayne Bay to Big Pine Key. They also survive within Everglades National Park.

Like turtles, crocodile females lay eggs in sand nests. The 20 to 50 or so eggs hatch from May to late July, when the eight- or nine-inch little ones crawl from the nest. They will continue to survive only with protection from crocodile hunters and the much greater threat of crocodile habitat destroyers.

> The law is quick to lock up the one
> who steals the goose from the common.
> But is quick to set the greater felon loose
> who steals the common from the goose.
>
> Author unknown (circa 1480)

Afterword

Kids living at the edge of the sea and far inland, too, have been letting everyone know how much the ocean means to them. Beach cleanups, whale-saving campaigns, and manatee adoptions all help protect life in the sea.

Admittedly, saving the ocean is probably more difficult than other environmental actions. We do not live on the surface of the sea, and we rarely dive into its depths. So the animals of the water world could vanish simply because we don't see what may be happening to them day to day. When was the last time you saw a whale? Have your eyes ever met those of a seal? Because we don't come in close contact with sea life, your work to let others know about ocean life is very valuable.

When whales were being hunted to near extinction, the constant educational efforts of many people, including kids, made others aware of the problem. Those educational efforts worked. So, too, can your efforts to let people know about vanishing sharks, endangered tunas, or threatened coastal habitats make a difference.

Try to pick some animals or some ocean habitats that mean a lot to you. Then work to protect these special species and places, using what you have learned in this book. Join with others, sharing ideas and projects. The National Audubon Society and other organizations welcome your participation in their efforts, too. Together, we can make sure the ocean is always home to great whales, sharks of many kinds, and the magnificent seabirds that fly from sea to shore.

As you choose some ocean-saving actions, remember that the entire world will be a better place for what you and your friends can do today. In your hands, our One Earth will be a better home for all life to share.

ONE EARTH

Index

A
Acadia National Park, 16
Algae, 2, 20
American oystercatchers, 23
Amphipods, 2
Angel sharks, 53
Antarctic convergence, 37
Anthony, Janet, 64–66
Auks, 28

B
Bald eagles, 6–12
Baleen whales, 37
Basking sharks, 53
Beach cleanups, 12–13
Bird Island, 29
Black oystercatchers, 23
Bluefin tuna, 48–49
Blue sharks, 53
Blue whales, 37–41, 44
Borja, Rodrigo, 44
Bowerman Basin, 64–66
Bowhead whales, 42
Brown, R.G.B., 29
Brown pelicans, 32–35

C
Cabrillo National Monument, 43
California otters, 19–20
Cape Canaveral, 5
Caribbean monk seals, 35
Carr, Archie, 61
Carson, Rachel, 7
CFCs (chlorofluorocarbons), 47
Chapman, Frank, 8
Chemicals, 32–34
Chesapeake Bay, 2, 5, 10
Coastal trees, 17
Coastal wetlands, 55–67
Coastal zone, 2, 4
Coast redwoods, 17
Colorado River, 32
Columbia River, 4, 38
Common terns, 30, 31
Convention on International Trade in Endangered Species, 61

Coral reefs, 49
Cottonwood, 17, 32
Crocodiles, 63, 67
Cumulative effects, 33–34

D
Dams, 38
DDT, 7–8, 33
Decoys, 25–26
Deforested shorelines, 3
Detritivores, 2
Detritus, 3
Dolphins, 37, 46
Dugong, 62

E
Eagle Geographics, 11
Eagles, 6–12, 16
Eastern Egg Rock Islands, 26
Endangered Species Act, 61
Endemic species, 50
Environmental Protection Agency, 13
Erosion, 4, 5
Eskimo curlews, 23
Estuaries, 2
Everglades National Park, 67
Exxon *Valdez*, 20, 28

F
Fin whales, 40
Fish and Wildlife Service, 9
Fishing line and nets, 13, 20
Food webs, 20
Forested shorelines, 1–17
Frillsharks, 54
Fur seals, 45–46

G
Galápagos Islands, 44
Garden products, 32, 34
Glossy ibis, 14
Grays Harbor, 64–66
Gray whales, 37, 40, 42–43
Great auks, 28
Great blue herons, 12–16
Great Gull Island, 29, 31
Great white sharks, 51–53
Greenland right whales, 42

Green sea turtles, 60
Gull predation, 30

H
Hands Across the Water project, 31
Harbor seals, 35
Hawaiian Islands, 35–36, 50
Hawksbill sea turtles, 60
Holdfast, 22
Horn sharks, 53
Humpback whales, 40, 43–45

I
International Whaling Commission, 43
Intertidal zones, 21
Inuit people, 42
Islands, 28–31, 35

J
Jellyfish, 59

K
Kelp, 19–22
Kemp's ridley sea turtles, 58–59
Keystone predators, 22, 50–51
Krill, 37

L
Large wading birds, 12–16
Leatherback sea turtles, 59–60
Leopard sharks, 53
Longline tuna gear, 47
Louisiana herons, 14

M
Machias Seal Island, 26
Manatees, 61–63
Mangrove forests, 3–4
Marine plants, 20
Marsh grasses, 2
Martha's Vineyard, 5
Megamouth sharks, 54
Mingan Island Cetacean Society, 42
Minke whales, 40
Mississippi River, 5, 38
Missouri River, 38
Monk seals, 35–36
Monofilament fishing line, 13
Muddy shorelines, 55–57, 64–66
Muir, John, 12

N
National Coalition Against the Misuse of Pesticides, 34
National Marine Fisheries Service, 58
Native Americans, 38, 42
Nesting beaches, 28–31, 33, 35
Nettleship, D. N., 29
Newport Beach, 4
Nooksack River delta, 4

O
Ocean depths, 54
Ocean vents, 54
Oil spills, 6–7, 20, 27–28
Olive ridley sea turtles, 57–58
Olympic National Park, 16, 17, 43
Open sea, 36–49
Orca whales, 43
Oystercatchers, 22–23
Ozone hole, 36, 47

P
Padre Island, 58
Palmer, Ralph, 15
Pelicans, 32–35
Penguins, 37
Pensacola Beach, 5
Peregrine falcons, 56, 64
Pesticides, 7–8, 33, 35
Phytoplankton, 20
Piping plovers, 27
Plastic netting, 45–46
Plastic trash, 12–13, 59–60
Plovers, 27
Pollution, 6–7, 12–13, 27–28, 32–35, 59–60
Pribilof Islands, 45
Puffins, 16, 24–28
Puget Sound, 2, 15–17, 35

R
Recycling, 12, 13
Reddish egrets, 14
Redwoods, 17
Right whales, 37, 42
Rio Brazos, 5
River otters, 19
Rocky coasts, 16, 18–28
Roseate spoonbills, 14
Roseate terns, 29–31

S
Salinity, 44
Salmon, 38
Salt marsh, 2, 20, 32
Sandpipers, 56
Sandy Hook, 5
San Francisco Bay, 2, 4, 55
San Juan Islands, 43
San Nicolas Island, 21
Scott, Bob, 21
Sculpins, 2
Seagrass, 2
Seals, 16, 35–37, 45–46
Sea minks, 19
Sea of Cortez, 32, 40
Sea otters, 16, 18–22
Sears, Richard, 39
Sea turtles, 57–61
Sea urchins, 22

Shannon Point, 4
Sharks, 49–54
Shorebirds, 56, 64
Shoreline forests, 1–17
Shoshone Indians, 38
Silent Spring (Carson), 7
Snake River, 38
Snowy egrets, 14
Spruce, 17
Stocks, 40
Stream monitoring, 52
Subtidal zones, 21

T
TED (turtle excluder device), 58
Terns, 29–31
Thresher sharks, 53
Tidepool monitoring, 51
Totoaba, 32

Trees, coastal, 17
Trout, 38
Tuna, 46–49

U
Urbana, Jorge, 41

W
Wading birds, 12–16
Water cycles, 32
Watersheds, 38
Wetlands, 55–67
Whales, 16, 37–45, 53–54
Whale sharks, 51
Whooping cranes, 14
Willow, 17

Z
Zooplankton, 20